ID889807

Matrons and Marginal Women
in Medieval Society

Matrons and Marginal Women in Medieval Society

EDITED BY

Robert R. Edwards and Vickie Ziegler

THE BOYDELL PRESS

First published 1995
The Boydell Press, Woodbridge

ISBN 0 85115 380 1

The Boydell Press is an imprint of Boydell & Brewer Ltd
PO Box 9, Woodbridge, Suffolk IP12 3DF, UK
and of Boydell & Brewer Inc.
PO Box 41026, Rochester, NY 14604–4126, USA

British Library Cataloguing-in-Publication Data
Matrons and Marginal Women in Medieval
Society
    I. Edwards, Robert R.   II. Ziegler,
Vickie L.
    305.42094
    ISBN 0–85115–380–1

Library of Congress Cataloging-in-Publication Data
Matrons and marginal women in medieval society / edited by
Robert R. Edwards and Vickie Ziegler.
    p.   cm.
Includes bibliographical references.
ISBN 0–85115–380–1
    1. Women – Europe – History – Middle Ages, 500–1500.
    I. Edwards, Robert, 1947–   . II. Ziegler, Vickie L.
. HQ1147.E85M381995
305.42'094'0902 – dc20   95–3838

This publication is printed on acid-free paper

Printed in Great Britain by
St Edmundsbury Press Ltd, Bury St Edmunds, Suffolk

Contents

Introduction

Over the last two decades, medieval studies, like every field within the humanities, has seen challenges to traditional methods and topics, to its procedures of scholarly investigation and its sense of what represents a useful object of study. In history these challenges have their origin early in the century, of course; but the effects on contemporary research can be seen in such developments as the return to narrative history, the application of ethnographic and anthropological models, and a heightened interest in not only diplomacy, politics, and official culture but also in the social life of groups on the periphery. In art history, the study of visual representation increasingly entails questions of ideology, power, and patronage as complements to iconography and stylistic concerns. Perhaps the greatest change has been felt in literary studies, where verbal artifacts are now seen as both poetic representations and discursive structures – as texts that simultaneously depict and interrogate reality. Post-structuralist, feminist, and historicist approaches have challenged formalist and humanist readings alike, and whatever the limitations of these new methods, their effect is widespread in contemporary scholarship.

The essays collected in this book draw from these challenges while preserving the strengths of traditional scholarship and criticism. Our general topic – the role of women within medieval society – divides its focus between matrons, who were recognized and integrated into official culture, and marginal women, who were countenanced more than condoned, though their social functions were obviously required. In the studies that follow, "matrons" refers to that diverse group of persons who could be collected under the phrase "honest women." We take the term marginal, as Barbara A. Hanawalt points out in her essay, to mean women situated outside the authorized roles that identify "honest women." They are marginal, then, not because of character but because of social function, and they include women of all sorts – religious laywomen as well as prostitutes – who are imagined as being on the periphery. The artistic and historical reality we intend to explore takes its shape from this tension between center and boundary.

The collection has its origin in an interdisciplinary conference on "Matrons and Marginal Women in Medieval Society," held at The Pennsylvania State University on April 5–7, 1991. The conference papers are presented here in revised form, and contributions from other scholars have been added to address topics that could not be covered in the original conference format. The essays reach across the disciplines of history, art history, and literary studies, but in a larger sense, they share a common concern with the nature of representation. The historians deal with a range of sources that record and depict the lives of matrons and marginal women, and their work addresses the cultural discourse brought to bear on these women as much as the actual experience of their lives. Similarly, the art historians and literary scholars deal at once with the portrayal of social roles and the ways in which artistic conventions and discursive practices condition representation.

Barbara A. Hanawalt's essay is a fitting opening to the collection, for it calls for a readjustment of Marxist and sociological definitions of marginality. Hanawalt proposes that these definitions, which have established the basic terms of inquiry, do not pay attention to gender as a determinant of marginality, and for her a key element in describing marginality is the concept of gendered space. Using documents such as coroners' inquests as well as literary sources, she identifies a pattern that confines women to regulated locales such as home and cloister. She then considers those groups of women, especially prostitutes and Beguines, who venture to the margins of gendered space. These groups, she argues, posed special problems for ecclesiastical and civil authorities, and the means of control employed to regulate them offer an important index to medieval social attitudes and cultural values.

Ann J. Kettle turns to another documentary source and a specific locale to study marginal women. In the fifteenth-century presentments made to the dean of the cathedral chapter at Lichfield, she finds represented the full apparatus of social regulation – its mechanisms, objects, and goals. Her essay traces how the practice of denunciation, as it was enforced in a late medieval provincial town, sought to control young servant girls (often immigrants, hence without protection of family) and full-time or occasional prostitutes so as to preserve the primacy of the family and of patriarchy, to regulate but not necessarily eradicate abuse by freemen, masters, and clergy. Domestic service, as Kettle points out, held the promise for some women of amassing their own dowries, conducting courtships on their own, and arranging marriages free from family interference. The visitation records show, however, the dark side – "seduction, illicit pregnancy, and sexual exploitation." In these records women are limited "by the suspicious attitude of the rest of society toward young unmarried women and by the dangers of sexual temptation and exploitation." At the same time, the records preserve traces of a lively social drama, in which false swearing usually won acquittal and official justice punished men and women who harbored and encouraged prostitutes but took little direct action against the women themselves.

James A. Brundage's essay examines a circumstance in which matrons, women at the presumed center of medieval social arrangements, approach the margins. On the death of their husbands, widows faced economic and social crisis, which threatened their property, children, and persons. Thus the issue of remarriage offers an avenue toward understanding the place of "honest women" and the designs of clerical culture to regulate them. Despite scriptural warrant, a second marriage was implicitly discouraged by clerical authorities in favor of renouncing sexuality altogether. Brundage points out that most medieval discussions of remarriage assume that the widow could exercise choice in deciding whether to remarry. The vantage point is that of elite and privileged women, when in fact most women were not in a favored group and had no practical choice but to remarry. Brundage analyzes the question of remarriage as an attempt "to accommodate the necessities of economic and social life among the majority of the widowed with the ascetic sexual ideals of the clerical elite." The disjunction between policy and practice that emerged in medieval society served no one well, he says, though on other occasions the canonists were alive to widows' plight. Brundage concludes, "The canon law concerning the remarriage of widows thus became an instrument for encouraging and fostering the renunciation of sexual pleasure and the affirmation of ascetic values."

In art history, the ideology of official culture is apparent in the fundamental conventions of representation. Laurinda S. Dixon's essay begins from retrospect with the representation of ailing women in seventeenth-century Dutch art, before the advent of Enlightenment science and social values. Dixon shows that these images draw on a tradition of medical learning that was itself shaped by ideological and social positions. Her review of the portrayal of women in medical texts offers a key to reading later artworks and the cultural suppositions that underlie them. In the medieval medical works ascribed to Trotula, for example, the Hippocratean concept of the "wandering womb," a trope conventionally used to express the stereotype of female hysteria, persists even in texts deeply indebted to Galenic tradition, which rejected the migrating "animal within the animal." In the final part of her essay, Dixon considers the much-debated sequence of miniatures in the thirteenth-century MS. Ashmole 377 in the Bodleian Library (Oxford), which she reads as a narrative representing the treatment of a female hysteric.

The literary studies in this collection approach our topic through the twin optic of history and poetry. The authors are concerned with how texts reflect historical conditions, but they believe that literary works are grounded as well in poetic tradition. Moreover, they suggest that the works, as forms of cultural production, also help to constitute historical conditions. Carol J. Clover examines the portrayal of maiden warriors in Old Norse literature as a convergence of poetic and social themes. Young women who were removed, at least temporarily, from marriage dress and take arms as men in a group of stories that form a subtype of the shield maiden theme. Clover rejects the psychoanalytic interpretations modern readers customarily attach to the materials and insists instead that the stories are a "fictional projection" that deserves to be understood anthropologically. The maiden warriors exist "between worlds," functioning as sons when male genealogy is interrupted, so that the generational succession of patriarchy can be maintained through feud and inheritance. Clover finds evidence for such roles in Icelandic law and in the social patterns of stateless societies where feud is the only mechanism for maintaining order. The compounding of fiction and history in the Norse stories, she concludes, is not a fantasy of female autonomy but a demonstration of the capacity of patrilineal society to enforce its social categories even when they appear to fall into contradiction.

Christopher Kleinhenz examines the interrelated themes of coming of age, rites of passage, and marriage in thirteenth-century Italian lyric. He notes that the women's voices expressed in the lyric create a number of personae: unhappy wives, women lamenting the loss of a husband or lover, full marriage partners, experienced wives, and young women longing for a husband or lover. The last of these he finds marginal in the dual sense that such women are both subordinated to patriarchy yet excluded from any compensatory status as a matron. Their "coming of age" as sexual, psychological, and social beings forces a transition to a new role within or beyond a sanctioned marriage. The lyrics that take this rite of passage as their dramatic moment are to be read, Kleinhenz insists, as literary texts rather than historical documents; for they reflect poetic conventions as well as social backgrounds, and the women who speak in and through them are imagined voices rather than authors. Nonetheless, the poems capture the pervasive tension between the individual and social structures. Kleinhenz's careful analysis of texts by Rinaldo d'Aquino and Cielo d'Alcamo shows the intricate negotiations of desire and power between the female speakers and their suitors.

Robert R. Edwards takes up a different kind of dramatized text – two speeches on marriage from Chaucer's *Canterbury Tales*. Focusing on the marriage encomium from the Merchant's Tale and the speech on marital equality in the Franklin's Tale, he shows how Chaucer's verbal artistry at once incorporates and challenges medieval traditions about marriage. The marriage encomium draws on authorities such as Eustache Deschamps, Albertanus of Brescia, and St. Jerome, and it describes marriage by defining the role of a wife. The doctrine that emerges in the speech is orthodox and unexceptionable, but it exists in a framework of dramatic and narrative irony. This balance between doctrine and poetic representation leaves the text open to competing interpretations that interrogate social relations. If the marriage encomium is essentially conservative, the speech from the Franklin's Tale seems to propose an innovative view of marriage that abolishes mastery in favor of reciprocity. Critics of the speech have claimed that it violates both doctrine and the events of the story, but Edwards finds that the problems of the speech are internal. They reside in the translation from Boccaccio's aristocratic world to the Franklin's bourgeois ethos and from classical male friendship to heterosexual marriage. Like the marriage encomium, the Franklin's speech is not merely an example of poetic ambiguity; it is a demonstration of the poet's capacity to question as well as portray.

No collection of essays can hope to survey the broad question of women's roles in the Middle Ages. We believe nonetheless that these studies isolate and examine crucial facets of the question. Our focus on "honest women" and their sisters on the margins shows, of course, the penetration of dominant ideology into social life and artistic representation. The examples of widows, maiden warriors, idealized wives, and marriage partners show the power of medieval social systems to establish roles and reinforce them through cultural production. So, too, do the examples of prostitutes, lay religious women, servant girls, and young women negotiating marriage and fulfillment. At the same time, they show the profound complexity of social categories in history and art. If medieval society is the origin of modern institutions such as marriage, the state, and the university, its legacy to us is not just social structures and cultural conventions but also the problems of understanding and value that surround them.

Carol J. Clover's essay originally appeared in the *Journal of English and Germanic Philology* (1986): 35–49, and a portion of Robert R. Edwards's essay is taken from an article published in *Speculum* 66 (1991): 342–67. They are included here with the kind permission of the editors of those journals. The editors of this collection thank Patricia A. Nickinson and Erik Schwab for their assistance. They also acknowledge with gratitude the support of the Institute for the Arts and Humanistic Studies; the Office of Research and the Graduate School; the College of the Liberal Arts, the College of Arts and Architecture; the Departments of History, Art History, German, English, French, Spanish, Classics, and Women's Studies; and the conference benefactors, supporters, and contributors: Dr. Helen R. Kearney, Kay Mills, Dr. Herberta Lundegren, Editha Adams, and Rick and Carole Sheviakov.

At the Margin of Women's Space in Medieval Europe*

Barbara A. Hanawalt

Marginals have constituted the newest social group in discussions of medieval society over the last two decades, beginning with Bronislaw Geremek's study of vagrants and other "low life" who lived in late medieval Paris.[1] With such a prestigious beginning, we might assume that a definition of what constituted marginality among medieval people is by now well established. To Geremek, who was working within a Marxist framework at the time he wrote his book, marginals were those people and groups who fell outside the social and economic or the legal and political categories that were acceptable to the mainstream of society. They may have been criminals, but they included bohemians and some clerks, tricksters, con-men, prostitutes, and even urban hermits. Geremek characterized their status by such attributes as having no settled home or family ties and being vagrants. Their place of association was the tavern. In the contemporary parlance they were of "no account" or "not of good fame,"[2] that is, they were not a part of the social and economic power structure. Such a definition of marginality contains a built-in, Marxist limitation, for it presumes that the only social marginals will be those who are at the bottom of society and regarded as morally reprehensible by the more fortunate classes.

A sociologist, Ephraim Mizruchi, worked toward a broader definition of marginality for medieval society which could include among the marginals such established groups as monks, apprentices, and Beguines, as well as prostitutes and criminals. His theory is based on a presumption that Europe had too many people to be assimilated into vacancies in the social networks. Medieval society developed institutions of social control that held the surplus in abeyance (that is,

*I thank Judith Bennett for reading drafts of this paper. I have delivered the paper at a number of places before publication and am grateful for comments from audiences at Dickenson College, The College of Wooster, The Institute of Historical Research at the University of London, and the Medieval Academy of America. Fellowship support during the writing of this paper came from the John Simon Guggenheim Foundation and the Wissenschaftskolleg zu Berlin.

[1] Bronislaw Geremek, *The Margins of Society in Late Medieval Paris*, trans. Jean Birrell (Cambridge: Cambridge University Press, 1987). First published in Polish in 1971 and in French in 1976.

[2] Geremek, particularly 270–99.

they slowed the integration process of the surplus by marginalizing them for a period of years in recognized institutions).[3] One cannot speak comfortably, however, about an excess of population in the century following the onset of plague in 1347. The fifteenth century was a demographic trough. Mizruchi's demographic evidence is from the sixteenth century and is projected back on medieval groups and institutions. Still, his inclusion of a larger variety of groups from different social classes as marginals is a move in the right direction.

Neither author views women as having a definition of marginality separate from men's. Their examples of marginality, prostitutes on the one hand and Beguines on the other, seem to our modern categories at opposite ends of the moral scale. The prostitute is a woman, married or single, who has slid into a transient life, selling her body, and assuming an outcast role in society in general. On the other hand, Beguines were single women who refused to accept such a demeaning role but sought instead to preserve their religious and moral integrity by forming communities of single women who led sober, pure lives outside a nunnery. They might eventually marry, or they might have devoted their earnings to the service of God and the poor throughout their lives. If we followed either Geremek or Mizruchi, we would agree that these are, in their own ways, marginals.

Modern discussions among feminist historians have centered on spheres of power, akin to Geremek's definition, which impose limitations on a discussion of marginality. This argument is that women's sphere of power is domestic while men's is public. Much has been written about patriarchy and the power that both church and secular law gave to men to restrict women from entering into the public sphere. Women's lack of access to magisterial ranks and higher market economies and the banning of women from universities, legal practice, and even most branches of medicine other than midwifery are well documented. All of these matters deal with power manipulations over women's access to economic, political, and intellectual spheres. But these categories apply more to the nineteenth century than they do to the Middle Ages, since women had virtually no access to the public arena. Placing marginal women into a discussion of spheres of influence becomes a useless exercise, because all women would fall into the excluded category. Within the domestic sphere, the analysis of power relations also does not identify the marginal women, since all women lived under patriarchy.

Those leading purveyors of patriarchal ideology, the medieval church hierarchy, regarded both prostitutes and Beguines as marginal women, but prostitutes were a necessary evil, whereas Beguines were an unusual threat as religious women outside traditional male control. Adultery, fornication, or any deviation from the preferred state of virginity or abstinence was unfortunate, but very likely to happen. Rather than having unbridled lust rampant among respectable lay and

---

[3] Ephraim H. Mizruchi, *Regulating Society: Beguines, Bohemians, and Other Marginals* (1983; Chicago: University of Chicago Press, 1987), particularly 8–27.

clerical men, prostitutes provided a convenient, limited locus for lust. Church authorities felt no moral dilemma in owning property on which organized brothels were located and collecting rents from such establishments. As we shall see, the real problem that they saw was in the prostitute who went unregulated into the community at large. Like city officials, they wanted to know and distinguish prostitutes from the rest of the female population. They wanted them geographically contained and officially sanctioned, but they did not strenuously object to their trade. On the other hand, the church authorities were very threatened by the pious, semi-secular Beguines. These women were virtually nuns, except for their refusal to live within the confines of monastic space and be directly answerable to a male ecclesiastical structure as cloistered nuns were. Their dwellings were among the poor or in secular households. Again, without an established spatial containment for these women, the male hierarchy was uncomfortable with their presence. Medieval concepts of marginal women, therefore, were not entirely akin to ours, and thus an exploration of what medieval men considered central in women's behavior and the space they could occupy are important to establish prior to a discussion of marginal women.

Centrality and marginality imply boundaries. I will argue, in this paper, that for medieval women the boundaries marked the physical space women could occupy. The exercise was less significant in separating respectable women and marginals than the spaces that they occupied. Women such as prostitutes and Beguines, who moved beyond the bounds of prescribed space, became marginals. By limiting the physical spaces that women could occupy and controlling women both within that space and outside of it, medieval men defined a spatial location for women that made women who moved beyond those boundaries more clearly marginal.

The questions that arise about women's restricted space help to form a definition of female marginality. Where could women go in conducting their admittedly limited social, political, and economic activities without male protection or censure? What did it mean when a woman stepped over these boundaries into a space beyond the pale, into the marginal area where respectable women could not venture unaccompanied or inappropriately attired (that is, not dressed in the symbols of their legitimate space)? For women to be physically unconstrained in mobility does not mean the same thing as it does for men. When they stepped out of their physical space, they were carrying an additional connotation of marginality. In the best of circumstances, and the Beguines are arguably that, women could not depart from a defined physical space without arousing more suspicion than men would in similar circumstances. A man in the late Middle Ages could be a mendicant friar living outside the walls of a monastic order, but a woman could not. Women who were in established prostitution houses or permissible areas were accepted, but the free-lance street walker was not.

Physical boundaries as well as moral and institutional ones are important in defining those who are inside and those who are on the margins, but Geremek, Mizruchi, and modern discussions of gendered power spheres do not refer to gendered space. For women to step outside physical boundaries and become transients, an aspect of Geremek's definition, connoted a moral lapse in itself. An example from the London Goldsmiths' Guild tells of the degradation implicit in removal of a female from the socially accepted space. William Rothely was fined "because he . . . against all humanity, sent his maid out of his house and suffered her to lie out two nights so she was fain to borrow money to lie at the Pewter Pot to the dishonor of all the fellowship [of goldsmiths]."[4] By expelling his servant from her protected physical space and forcing her to stay at an inn, Rothely had disgraced himself and his guild. A more extreme example is Joan of Arc who moved beyond the woman's space and dress into the male realm of battlefield and armor. In forming a definition of marginal women, therefore, we must look beyond the usual issues of patriarchal constraints over women's spheres of influence to the actual physical constraints on women's movements.

It is to anthropologists that we owe the observation that women's access to the entire environment was restricted. Pierre Bourdieu observed among the Berbers not only the division of the house into male and female space but also the value judgments associated with this division. This led to a more generalized observation that the power of dominant groups lies, in part, in their ability to control the ordering of space for subservient groups.[5] Daphne Spain has done an extensive survey of household space but has not applied her analysis to preindustrial Europe.[6] Martine Segalen's exploration of the division of male and female space among the French peasants is valuable because she brings her observations to a rural European situation. She notes that there was "a female *house*" and "a male *outside*." When women went outside the house, they did so in the company of other women. Men's space was the fields. Thus, she observed, not only were tasks divided in the peasant communities, but also the allocation of space.[7] Traditional European society did not have space (outside of some sacred areas such as monasteries) that absolutely excluded either sex. Men did not congregate alone in taverns or temples, and women were not kept in women's quarters or harems. Women did work in fields at harvest, and men lived in the houses. Nonetheless, strong custom dictated how women moved in the spaces that men dominated. To break these rules, as Mary Douglas observed, made women become "polluting" and "dangerous."[8] Thus, as we shall see, women who broke the codes limiting their movement outside their allotted physical space were subject to harassment.

---

4   T. F. Reddaway, *The Early History of the Goldsmiths' Company, 1327–1509* (London: Edward Arnold, 1975), 151.

5   Pierre Bourdieu, *Outline of a Theory of Practice*, trans. Richard Nice (Cambridge: Cambridge University Press, 1977), 90–91, 160–63.

6   Daphne Spain, *Gendered Spaces* (Chapel Hill: University of North Carolina Press, 1992).

7   Martine Segalen, *Mari et femme dans la société paysanne*, Bibliothèque d'ethnologie historique (Paris: Flammarion, 1980). In her *Historical Anthropology of the Family*, trans. J. C. Whitehouse and Sarah Matthews (Cambridge: Cambridge University Press, 1986), 205–12, 218–19, she extends the observation to other preindustrial classes.

8   Mary Douglas, *Purity and Danger* (London: Routledge and Kegan Paul, 1966), 140–58, discusses the interplay between men and women and ideas about pollution. Victor Turner, *The Ritual Process: Structure and Anti-Structure* (New York: Aldine, 1969), 109–11 has spoken about the perceived danger of the weak in societies.

Lest we think that spatial limitation on women was only a preindustrial phenomenon, consider the many places that a Victorian woman could not go: whole city districts, taverns, many offices, social clubs, and so on. Consider the comments that women get today when they enter men's bars or even the physical abuse they may suffer if they enter "male space," such as locker rooms. Modern men would argue, quite correctly, that they too suffer ridicule upon entering "women's space." If some of the boundaries between proper and marginal space for women have been removed over the centuries, they are hardly entirely gone.

Defining the physical space: the proper arena for matrons

For ordinary women early socialization reinforced by moral precepts in advice books and sermons contributed to a spatial identity and an early awareness of the consequences of marginalization. As one would assume, it was not only male preachers who taught women their spatial identity. Children learned very young, at their parents' knees, about gendered space. Medieval coroners' inquests into accidental death clearly show that by the age of two and three more female children died in the house and about the hearth than did male children. The female children identified early with their mothers' work pattern and died tipping pots of hot liquid on themselves or getting too near the hearth, while male children followed their fathers outside and drowned in ditches.[9]

Playing upon the mother's role in socialization were such poems as "How the Good Wife Taught Her Daughter" in which the daughter is told that her place is the home and that she should keep her eyes down when she is in the streets. The poem carefully spells out the dangers of public places.

> An wan thou goist in the way, go thou not to faste,
> Braundishe not with thin heed, thi schuldris thou ne caste;
> Haue thou not to manye wordis; to swere be thou not leefe,
> For alle such maners comen to an yuel preef:
> For he that cacchith to him an yuel name,
> It is to him a foule fame,
> Mi leue childe.

Further warnings about behavior out of the house include not getting drunk in taverns, not going house to house buying beer after selling your cloth, and not accompanying your lover to places where he might be able to seduce you. Finally, the good daughter would not go to shows like a common strumpet but "wone at hom, daughtir, and loue thi werk myche."[10] Equivalent moral poems for men caution against appearing too frequently in taverns, but they suggest meeting the

---

[9] Barbara A. Hanawalt, *The Ties That Bound: Peasant Families in Medieval England* (New York: Oxford University Press, 1986), 180–82.

[10] *The Babees Book. . .*, ed. Frederick J. Furnivall, EETS OS 32 (London: N. Trübner & Co., 1868), 36–47.

eyes of others on the street to show a good quality of deportment. Women are to preserve their private space in cities by keeping their heads down, but men are to use the streets as an arena for impressing others.

In Florence bourgeois girls were more literally isolated, thus giving them an early sense of limited space. At the age of six or seven their fathers enrolled them in convents where they would stay until they were married at about age sixteen or where they would take the nun's veil at about the age of twelve. Boys, on the other hand, remained at home and went to secular schools.[11]

Books of advice for rearing noble girls emphasized carefully guarded seclusion, and, obviously, bourgeois literature imitated these. While girls should be taught to read, write, and pray in addition to sewing and weaving, isolation was to be reinforced by teaching them silence along with chastity, modesty, and humility. Nothing can be more spatially confining than enforced silence in which the very escape of words puts the speaker in a marginal category. Giles of Rome enjoined lessons in silence and physical seclusion of noble girls. Seclusion was still an important characteristic of women's education in the Renaissance. Vives, the Renaissance expert on educating women, devoted more chapters to guarding and teaching noble girls to limit their social participation than to their literary or household skills.[12] Male advisers of noble women realized that these women would have to appear in public even though they did not consider it desirable. If they had to leave their homes, then they should do so appropriately accompanied and keep their eyes down to insure that they did not participate, by eye contact, in public space.[13]

Moral injunctions had long criticized women who dared to move outside their space. The synod of Nantes in 895, for instance, condemned women who "with barefaced impudence" pleaded in general assemblies and public meetings:

> It is indecent and even reprehensible, even among barbarians, for women to discuss the cases of men. Those who should be discussing their woolen work and weaving with the residents of women's quarters should not usurp

---

[11] Christiane Klapisch-Zuber, *Women, Family, and Ritual in Renaissance Italy*, trans. Lydia Cochraine (Chicago: University of Chicago Press, 1985), 109.

[12] Vincent of Beauvais, *De Eruditione Filiorum Nobilium*, ed. A. Steiner, Medieval Academy of America Publications 32 (Cambridge, Mass.: Medieval Academy of America, 1938), 172–219. Giles of Rome, *De Regimine Principum* (Augsburg, 1473), Bk. 2, pt. 2, chs. 19–21. All of these are quoted in Nicholas Orme, *From Childhood to Chivalry: The Education of the English Kings and Aristocracy 1066–1530* (London: Methuen, 1984), 106–7, 235. See also Ruth Kelso, *Doctrine for the Lady of the Renaissance* (Urbana: University of Illinois Press, 1956), 53, with a recommendation that the young girl remain in her father's house and not go out into the world.

[13] Alice A. Hentsch, ed., *De la littérature didactique du moyen âge s'adressant spécialement aux femmes* (1903; reprint, Geneva: Slatkine Reprints, 1975), 91 (Matfre Ermengau, 1288), 105 (Francesco da Barberino, 1309), 173 ("Castigos y doctrinas que un sabio dava a sus hijas," fifteenth century).

the authority of senators in public meetings just as if they were palace officials.[14]

Not content with limiting the space that women were to occupy and their behavior when they moved out of that space, male moralists also imposed regulations on what women were to wear. Dress codes are, of course, another way of confining women – in this case within an outer layer of cloth. The nun's veil is the most apparent of the dress codes, but in London and many cities of Europe, city fathers regulated headdress:

> No woman of the town shall henceforth go to market nor into the highway out of her house with a hood furred with budge, whether it be of lamb or of conies, upon pain of forfeiting her hood to the use of the Sheriffs, except dames who wear furred capes the hoods of which bear fur such as they wish. . . . Brewsters, nurses, other servants, and women of disreputable character adorn themselves and wear hoods furred with *gros veer* and miniver after the manner of reputable women.[15]

Not only headdress but a variety of clothing items determined the properly clad woman in public.[16]

The obverse of city regulation for respectable women was the clothing signifiers that cities prescribed for prostitutes. In London a hood of multi-colored cloth and in southern France sleeves and headdress distinguished prostitutes. Italy prohibited prostitutes from wearing veils or mantels like respectable women and required them to wear a yellow strip denoting their trade.[17] Perhaps the moralists most preoccupied with women's dress were those advising noble women on proper courtly attire for keeping spatial decorum in public. *Der Waelsche Gast*, an early thirteenth-century moral poem, contains a long description indicating how a woman can ride a horse so that her mantel completely enshrouds her: "no part of her body can be discovered." This type of advice was international in character, for it also appears in Robert de Blois's *Le Chastoiement des Dames*, among other authorities.[18] Many factors entered into men's attempts to regulate

---

[14] Suzanne Fonay Wemple, *Women in Frankish Society: Marriage and the Cloister 500 to 900* (Philadelphia: University of Pennsylvania Press, 1985), 105–6.

[15] *Calendar of Letter-Books Preserved Among the Archives of the Corporation of the City of London, 1275–1487, Letter Book A*, 11 vols. (A-L), ed. Reginald Sharpe (London: John Edward Francis, 1889), 220.

[16] Diane Owen Hughes, "Distinguishing Signs: Ear-rings, Jews and Franciscan Rhetoric in the Italian Renaissance City," *Past and Present* 112 (1986): 3–59.

[17] Ruth Mazo Karras, "The Regulation of Brothels in Later Medieval England," *Signs* 14 (1989): 421; reprint in *Sisters and Workers in the Middle Ages*, ed. Judith M. Bennett, Elizabeth A. Clark, Jean F. O'Barr, B. Anne Vilen, and Sarah Westphal-Wihl (Chicago: University of Chicago Press, 1989), 122; Leah Otis, *Prostitution in Medieval Society: The History of an Urban Institution in Languedoc* (Chicago: University of Chicago Press, 1985), 80; Jacques Rossiaud, *Medieval Prostitution*, trans. Lydia G. Cochrane (Oxford: Basil Blackwell, 1988), 64–65; Hughes, 29–30.

[18] Hentsch, *De la littérature didactique*, 52–53, 75–77, and throughout Hentsch's collection of didactic literature for women.

female dress. In part, they wished to maintain control over signs of social class so that only wives and daughters of the right sort could wear fine furs and appear in public properly escorted. In part, the city fathers felt that women in prostitution should wear a sign of their trade by way of truth in advertising as well as establishing social distinctions. But the veiling, hooding, and capping of women also served a similar purpose to veiling in Islamic society. Women could walk outside their homes in the privacy of their own space, surrounded by veils or hoods that both limited a view of them and their view of the outside world. Blinded as horses were, they were less likely to stray from the straight and narrow path.

If women's exterior space was regulated, so too might their interior physical space be, particularly if they were pursuing a religious life. The ideal of total virginity was described in terms of objects with walls and physical boundaries – a jewel, treasure, a sacred vessel. Jerome puts the choice of defending the internal space graphically, as usual: "Go not out from home, nor wish to behold the daughters of a strange country. . . . Diana went out and was ravished." Those virgins who went out to "seek a bridegroom in the highways" will suffer a similar fate. Such a fallen virgin "shall be stripped and her hinderparts shall be bared in her own sight."[19] The language of spiritual virginity, therefore, might also be couched in terms of private space and its loss in terms of exposure in public space.

Was women's space the moralists' myth?

One could argue that the parameters of women's space were all in the minds of moralists and that in real life women did not limit their movements to the confines of house, castle, village, and urban quarter. Historical evidence, however, indicates that women did indeed spend the larger part of their lives within prescribed spaces. Record evidence and literature speak to a general social consciousness about gendered space. My argument reaches beyond the traditions of the ancient and Carolingian world in which some women were confined to the *gynaeceum* either as slaves or serfs for a period of their lives, where they would work together producing cloth. They were carefully protected and had their separate living quarters in the compound with their workshop.[20] Segalen's observations about the space of a peasant woman's sphere of activity receives confirmation from the study of accidental deaths recorded in fourteenth-century English coroners' inquests. Medieval coroners, like modern ones, were charged with investigating all cases of violent death. Thus their duty was to inquire about all homicides, suicides, and misadventures. The inquests can, at their fullest, provide a wealth of detail that gives the reader a sense of being at the scene of the tragedy. The inquests that I used gave the name of the accused; the date and sometimes the

---

[19] Jane Tibbets Schulenburg, "The Heroics of Virginity: Brides of Christ and Sacrificial Mutilation," in *Women in the Middle Ages and the Renaissance: Literary and Historical Perspectives*, ed. Mary Beth Rose (Syracuse: Syracuse University Press, 1986), 32–33.

[20] David Herlihy, *Opera Muliebria: Women and Work in Medieval Europe* (New York: McGraw-Hill, 1990), 34–38.

time of day of the accident; sometimes the age of the victim; and usually the place, activity, and instrument that caused the death.

In rural coroners' inquests, which reflect the life of the peasants, I had one thousand adult males and females for whom a clear place of accident could be established; the differences were striking. Only twelve percent of the men compared to thirty percent of the women died in their homes. Private property such as a neighbor's house or close, tavern, manor house, and so on were the place of death of only six percent of the men but nine percent of the women. In public areas within the village such as greens, streets, highways, churches, and markets again women predominated with twenty-two percent of their accidents there compared to men's eighteen percent. But if we look at fields, marl pits, forests, and so on, we find that thirty-eight percent of the men have accidents there, while only eighteen percent of the women do. Likewise, men had four percent more of their accidents in waterways. The aggregate picture is more dramatic than the breakdown into various categories. Women had sixty-one percent of their accidents within their home and village, while men had only thirty-six percent in this limited area.

Peasant women's daily rounds of activities within their sphere reflect the reason for such spatial limitation: thirty-seven percent of their activities were related to maintaining and provisioning the household. These activities included food preparation, laundry, brewing, getting water, starting fires, collecting fruits, and working with domestic animals. The other major activity (thirty percent) that involved women in accidents were related to transportation such as walking. For men, transportation was the highest (forty-three percent), and this category included carting, horse back riding, and boating in addition to walking. The pursuit of agriculture and construction, however, show men's greater range of mobility: nineteen percent of men compared to four percent of women died pursuing agriculture; and eleven percent of the men, and no women, died in construction related accidents.[21]

To translate the numerical picture of women's as opposed to men's space into a visual picture, imagine a village in late February or March when the plowing for summer crops was in progress. At mid-morning, the men and boys of eight and above will be out in the fields. The men will be plowing and the boys goading the ox or taking care of the village herds. The only men in the village will be the priest and perhaps an infirm man or two. It is no wonder that the priests had a reputation for lechery akin to that of the mid-twentieth-century milkman, since they were the only vital males who occupied women's space while the men were in the fields. Those occupying the village streets, tavern (with the alewife attendant), closes, and houses will be women and small children. Women will be found in the fields when necessity demands it: when there are no boys to goad the ox, when field work such as weeding or harvesting requires all hands to turn out, or when girls replace boys as herders. During the midday meal and after vespers, the streets, greens, and closes will also contain the male population.

---

21 Hanawalt, *The Ties That Bound*, see tables 271.

The abandonment of house and village space to women during the day was a source of anxiety on the part of peasant males, not simply because the village priest had license to roam freely. Most peasant societies have a version of the tale in which the husband accuses his wife of spending her day gossiping at the tavern rather than working hard, as he does in the field. He proposes that they change places for the day. The emphasis on "changing places" rather than roles is significant. Medieval England had its version that is called the "Ballad of the Tyrannical Husband." The good wife warns him that her day started earlier than his, for she rose to nurse the baby and start the fire. She then milked the cows and took them to pasture, and made butter and cheese while she watched the children and dried their tears. Next she fed the poultry and took the geese to the green. She baked and brewed every fortnight, and worked on carding wool, spinning, and beating flax. Her husband is insistent, and they change places, claiming that her work was easy by comparison to his. Although our manuscript is incomplete, the denouement to the tradition is that when the wife returns from plowing, she finds the children crying, the beer spoiled, the cow not milked, and the husband defeated. He returns to the fields and she to the house and village.[22]

Even though peasant women had the daily use of house and village, their legal control over this environment was limited. As a wife, a woman shared the property with her husband, but he had the legal control over it. As a widow, she had dower rights to a portion of the land but only for her lifetime, and she could not alienate it. A woman might control some land in her own right by purchase, gift, or inheritance; but the quantity tended to be small unless she was an heiress, and in any case her husband gained control on marriage.[23] Thus, the domination over usage of space was different from a political or legal control of it.

In the commission of crime, women also stayed near their homes. Their crimes were concentrated in burglary, larceny, and the receiving of stolen property of known felons. The first two crimes were most likely to be committed against neighbors in the same village, and the last was, of course, a crime committed in their own home. It was the men who committed crimes in the fields, forests, and highways.[24] Likewise, women were more likely to be victims of homicide in their homes or villages rather than in the fields.[25] If we look at the landscape of Europe today for evidence of women's use of space, we will find it in the villages rather than the fields. The ridges and furrows that create a washboard effect on the land, particularly when seen in aerial photographs, are peasant men's legacy, but in

---

[22] *Reliquiae Antiquae: Songs and Carols*, ed. Thomas Wright and James O. Halliwell (London: Percy Society, 1841), 2: 196–99.

[23] Judith M. Bennett, *Women in the Medieval English Countryside: Gender and Household in Brigstock Before the Plague* (New York: Oxford University Press, 1987), ch. 2.

[24] Barbara A. Hanawalt, *Crime and Conflict in Medieval Communities, 1300–1348* (Cambridge, Mass.: Harvard University Press, 1979), 120–22, 168–70.

[25] In general women were not cited as victims of property crimes because their property, unless they were single or widows, belonged to their husbands. For the pattern on homicide, see James B. Given, *Society and Homicide in Thirteenth-Century England* (Stanford: Stanford University Press, 1977), 169.

deserted villages and in archaeological sites, the U-shaped depressions mark the location of a former house floor formed by the sweeping of a housewife's broom.[26]

Noble women were no more immune from spatial limitations than were peasants and serfs. While they might travel extensively, their space and sphere of activity were still the domestic arena. For some noble women, the castle was more of a cell than a home. The Duchess of Brunswick told her priest that after her hard life, she expected to go directly to heaven. The priest reacted with disbelief:

> "That would be a marvel. You were born in a fortress and bred in castles and for many years now you have lived with your husband, the Lord Duke, ever in midst of manifold delights, with wine and ale, meat and venison; and yet you expect to fly away to heaven directly you die." She answered, "Beloved father, why should I not now go to heaven? I have lived here in this castle like an anchoress in a cell. What delights or pleasures have I enjoyed here, save that I have made shift to show a happy face to my servants and gentlewomen? I have a hard husband (as you know) who has scarce any care or inclination toward women. Have I not been in this castle even as it were in a cell?"[27]

For the Duchess, the privileged space had brought not happiness but confinement.

For most noble women the routine of the castle or manor house was one of management. The English queen's household books or even those of a more modest establishment such as that of Dame Alice de Bryene of Acton Hall in Suffolk show days filled with accounting for household supplies, managing servants, feeding guests and retinue, and perhaps managing estates as well.[28]

The sister of Henry III, Eleanor of Montefort, played an active role in her husband's rebellion against her brother, but her political activism consisted of entertaining partisans at the various castles that they controlled. Occasionally, a woman might also be called upon to defend the castle against attack, as Margaret Paston did against those who claimed that the property belonged to them.[29]

If we are to imagine the castle as women's space, as we imagined the village, we would not find the environment devoid of men. Most of the household staff, including servants, grooms, officials, and members of the lord's affinity, were present at the castle even if the lord was away.[30] The woman's space would be the chamber of the castelaine and the dormitory for the single women in her charge.

[26] Guy Beresford, *The Medieval Clay-Land Village: Excavations at Glotho and Barton Blont* (London: Society for Medieval Archaeology, 1975), 27–29.

[27] Johannes Busch, *Liber de Reformatione Monasteriorum*, ed. Karl Grube, Geschichtsquellen der Provinz Sachsen (Halle, 1886), 779, as quoted by Eileen Power, *Medieval Women* (Cambridge: Cambridge University Press, 1975), 36.

[28] *The Household Book of Dame Alice de Bryene of Acton Hall Suffolk, Sept. 1412–Sept. 1413*, trans. M. K. Dale (Ipswich: Suffolk Institute of Archaeology and History, 1931). Margaret Wade Labarge, *A Baronial Household of the Thirteenth Century* (Totowa, N.J.: Barnes and Noble, 1965) for the house of Eleanor de Montefort.

[29] Power, *Medieval Women*, 45.

[30] Kate Mertes, *The English Noble Household, 1250–1600* (Oxford: Basil Blackwell, 1988), 56–59.

She would have her female companions and personal servants. The management of the castle would be the concern of the castelaine, but, as with the peasant woman, she did not have legal control over it. As long as she had a husband or son, legal disposition over her space was not in her power.

Literary parallels confirm the spatial location of noble women as they do with peasants. Penny Gold has observed in *The Lady and the Virgin* that the action involving women in the *chansons de geste* always occurs at home. Segments involving men occur in battlefields, courts, or forests; but when the plot features a woman, the action shifts to the castle. In *The Song of William*, for instance, Guiburc plays a heroic role supporting ties of kinship in her family, giving comfort at home, and inspiring her husband and male kin to assert themselves on the battlefield. As Gold points out, "The spatial structure of this epic provides us with a framework for an analysis of the role of women. . . . The male sphere of action and the female sphere of action are clearly separated geographically (with the men, but not the women, present in both spheres)."[31] The real life position of twelfth-century noble French women, as revealed in charters involving gifts of land, indicate that their role was similar to that portrayed in the *chansons de geste*.[32]

Conservative medieval social theorists recognized three social orders: those who worked (peasants), those who fought (nobles), and those who prayed (clergy). Women were classified into those three categories as well. While priesthood was denied to women, those who wanted a life of prayer became nuns and anchorites. For these women their geographical space was closely defined – the nunnery and the anchorite's solitary cell. The early advice for claustration of nuns shows the profound concern for isolating women within a defined and secluded place. Caesarius of Arles recommended that "if a girl leaving her parents, desires to renounce the world and enter the holy fold to escape the jaws of the spiritual wolves by the help of God, she must never, up to the time of her death, go out of the monastery." A ninth-century rule, perhaps based on Jerome, was even more graphic: "let your convent become your tomb, where you will be dead and buried with Christ."[33] Convent life was not a common choice for medieval women. Entry into a convent required a dowry that was beyond the means of the peasantry. The institutions were, therefore, made up of women of the gentry and noble ranks. At no period was there a large number of nuns. Eileen Power concluded that at its height, around 1350, only 3,500 women occupied the nunneries in England.[34] In other words, conventional nunneries were not the place that society could conveniently shelve, in Mizruchi's terms, an excess female population.

For the nuns, however, the space within the walls was largely their own. The

---

[31] Penny Schine Gold, *The Lady and the Virgin: Image, Attitude, and Experience in Twelfth-Century France* (Chicago: University of Chicago Press, 1985), 5, 10, 14–15.

[32] Gold, ch. 4.

[33] Schulenburg, "The Heroics of Virginity," 42.

[34] Power, *Medieval Women*, 89–96.

offices of Sacristan, Chambress, and Cellaress were all filled by nuns, as, of course, was that of abbess. All nunneries had to rely on the spiritual services of a priest or chaplain, and the larger ones might also employ men for work around the nunnery. But the cloister, dormitory, refectory, and chapter house were reserved for the women to pray, work, and play. Nonetheless, the cloistered area was secured and enforced by bishops or by male-dominated superiors in orders such as Dominicans or Franciscans. Literary parallels again suggest that concepts of women's space entered into the consciousness of medieval people; Chaucer's prioress is accompanied outside her convent with the appropriate escort of a priest and nuns. But even with this escort, Madame Eglentyne was a subject of "worldly" satire.

The anchorite's cell was even more restricted as a physical space than the nunnery. Anchorites did not necessarily withdraw into the wilderness but lived in cells in parish churches, castles, and even great monasteries such as Westminster. These women hermits (there were men as well) were popular figures and could rely upon the laity and clergy for food, clothing, and a cell in the local church in exchange for prayers for their benefactors. Women who undertook this particularly severe confinement had little or no latitude for movement.[35] Even when they chose an urban environment, their position was marginal in terms of their confinement outside the mainstream. Spatially confined, the worst threat they offered was either local gossip or major visionary experiences (Julian of Norwich). They did not wander about the streets and preach or live outside strictly controlled space.

The urban environment and the urban population were not a part of the original medieval conception of tri-partite social organization. The growth of urban centers in the twelfth century and their continued dynamic presence in Europe presented new challenges to classifying social stratification. Artisans fit into the old category of those who worked with their hands, but the merchants who made a profit from investment and could equal or rival the nobility in wealth and taste were a difficult group to classify. Among the novel problems that the new environment presented was a definition of women's space. Women and men were continually mixed together in the urban environment with the home serving as the shop or business headquarters and men and women mixing in the market place. Men's space and women's could not be so easily separated as they were in village and castle. Homicide statistics indicate that, while urban women were more likely to meet with violence in their own homes, more were killed in streets and in other people's homes or taverns than in the rural environment. Furthermore, women were more likely to be killed alone, whereas in the country they were more often in the company of a relative.[36]

Even with this greater homogeneity of the sexes, women still moved within a

---

[35] See Ann K. Warren, *The Anchorites and Their Patrons in Medieval England* (Berkeley and Los Angeles: University of California Press, 1985) for a good discussion of the institution of anchorites.

[36] Given, *Society and Homicide*, 179–83.

narrower confine of the urban environment than did men. Marriages were, by preference, made within the quarter or neighborhood, partly because people of similar social status or occupation lived in these quarters.[37] The daily rounds of activities in the London coroners' inquests into accidental deaths also indicate that women's activities were centered in their homes. For women the home and garden area were the major places of death (fifty percent) with the streets being the location of thirty percent of their deaths. No women died in shops or workplaces and only ten percent on the wharves or in the river. Men, however, had the majority of their fatal accidents in the river or wharf area (thirty percent), street (eighteen percent), and shop and workplace (sixteen percent), but only twenty percent in the home.[38] Literature again provides examples of the uneasiness of males when urban women moved outside the city quarter. Chaucer's Wife of Bath is both a much-travelled and much-ridiculed woman. Her honor is questioned because she travelled beyond Bath.

In the religious life, the urban environment also presented new opportunity. As we have observed, Beguines were women who did not have the wealth to join a nunnery but who wanted to live a life of poverty and chastity in urban communities where they made their meager living by their labor, usually at spinning. Italian, French, and Flemish cities had these groups of single, pious laywomen who lived, uncloistered, among the urban poor.[39] Like anchorites, they were marginal because they were outside the normal control of cloister and home, but to the church authorities they were more of a threat because they were outside the spatial control of the cell. These were unconfined women, alone or only in the company of other women in urban space.

At the other end of the moral scale, as we have observed, were the prostitutes who plied their trade in the urban environment and were not initially confined to a particular space. These women escaped the strictures of confinement to household and shop and, unlike respectable women, did not keep their eyes down when they were in the street but openly invited invasion of their physical, bodily space. In this respect they were between respectable women who were not to make eye contact in order to preserve private space and men who were to look about them in order to dominate the public space. Prostitutes looked about them and made eye contact in order to invite invasion of private space. Streets were an arena for

[37] Klapisch-Zuber, *Women, Family, and Ritual in Renaissance Italy*, 81, shows that marriages were usually among the *gonfalone*, a subdivision of the quarter, in Florence unless the family was undergoing social mobility either up or down.

[38] The total sample size is 267 accidental deaths from 1275 to 1341. Cases appear in Reginald R. Sharpe, *Calendar of Coroners' Rolls of the City of London, A.D. 1300–1378* (London: Richard Clay and Sons, 1913); Public Record Office Just. 2/94–A; and *Calendar of Letter-Books of the City of London, Letter Book B*, ed. Reginald R. Sharpe (London: John Edward Francis, 1900), 256–80.

[39] Brenda M. Bolton, "Mulieres Sanctae," in *Women in Medieval Society*, ed. Susan Mosher Stuard (Philadelphia: University of Pennsylvania Press, 1976), 141–56; and Ernest W. McDonnell, *The Beguines and Beghards in Medieval Culture* (New Brunswick: Rutgers University Press, 1954).

a variety of spatial contacts depending on the gender or profession of the sojourner.

Spatial confinement in medieval society was not necessarily a safe haven for women. While the allocation of guarded space to upper-class women provided security, women who served as slaves or domestics could find the confined space one that permitted physical violation and violence without recourse to public intervention. Spatial segregation did not mean security from violence, as homicide figures show. In the case of slaves, they could neither remain chaste because of the abuse of masters nor could they escape the house because they were forced to remain celibate. Servants, on the other hand, planned to work for a limited number of years until they had accumulated enough money for a dowry and marriage.[40] Even so, they might be effectively reduced to concubinage or pay with their bodies as well as their labor for their wages.

Single women also worked as wage laborers and sometimes apprentices in various crafts. They worked with cloth making, silver and gold thread or lace production, and in victualing trades. If the girl were an apprentice, she would live in the same house as her master and work in the adjoining shop. If she were a day laborer, her space would be that of the shop and her home. In any case, the work function would be performed in a familial environment. Once married, urban women of the artisanal crafts would most likely become part of the production force of their husband's trade, or they would enter the victualing business that could be carried out from their own homes. For the upper class women, those married to the merchant elite, home would be the chief center of their lives.

Only widows of craftsmen and merchants, or in London married women acting as *femme sole*, ventured into the broader market place or dealt in substantial production. But even here, they were limited to their own cities. They could not accompany their goods to trade fairs or other towns.[41] In the urban environment, therefore, the home, either natal or that of a master, was the chief place of living and work for urban women where they worked in the same environment with men. Their relationship to more public places such as churches, streets, markets, guildhalls, and taverns was similar to that of the peasant woman's relationship to the village. Since the space was shared with men, urban women had more injunctions about behavior in public that would preserve a space around them. But the homogeneous environment gave more scope to single women such as prostitutes and Beguines.

---

[40] Christiane Klapisch-Zuber, "Women Servants in Florence during the Fourteenth and Fifteenth Centuries," in *Women and Work in Preindustrial Europe*, ed. Barbara A. Hanawalt (Bloomington: Indiana University Press, 1986), 56–80. See also Susan Mosher Stuard, "To Town to Serve: Urban Domestic Slavery in Medieval Ragusa," 39–55, in the same collection of essays.

[41] Katheryne L. Reyerson, "Women in Business in Medieval Montpellier," 117–44; Maryanne Kowaleski, "Women's Work in a Market Town: Exeter in the Late Fourteenth Century," 145–60; and Martha C. Howell, "Women, the Family Economy, and the Structures of Market Production in Cities of Northern Europe during the Late Middle Ages," 198–222 in *Women and Work in Preindustrial Europe*.

Keeping women in their space

In taking up once again the issue of space and exercising power over it, we must think again of the arguments of Pierre Bourdieu that domination of space means regulation of those within it. Medieval men consciously strove through a variety of mechanisms to keep women within their space and to regulate them within that designated area. Since they regarded women by their very nature as unruly, the best way to control them was to enclose them. Male kin, ecclesiastical authorities, and masters all undertook to insure that their female dependents were either properly maintained in their homes or were appropriately attired and escorted when they were away from that designated space. Single women were the chief concern of the official male establishment because married women were under the regulation of their husbands, and presumably they would take measures to restrict their wives and daughters. Nuns, Beguines, and prostitutes, however, posed a threat to the male establishment so that they had to be controlled.

Regulations were an obvious way to curtail women's access to greater public space, but moral injunctions, ridicule, and outright attacks were used as well. Women who strayed from their designated space might be subject to sexual assault because they were neither under the protection of a responsible male nor were they in their accustomed space. Again, lest we think that these injunctions on women's mobility are outmoded, consider the risks a woman encounters in entering an all-male pool hall in modern America.

Challenges to spatial domination occurred continually throughout the Middle Ages. Every new monastic movement brought a flood of women anxious to take vows. Charismatic preachers converted pious women to their cause. The Premonstratensian and Cistercian orders found themselves embarrassed by large numbers of women who wanted to join their orders. Their response was to limit the number accepted and severely enclose them. The revolutionary, mendicant order of Francis of Assisi also attracted women, but Innocent III was quick to insure that they would be under strict claustration rather than begging as did the Friars. Thus the Poor Clares became a convent group like other nuns.[42] Beguines, as we have seen, formed a separate problem because they resisted claustration. It took a combination of a papal prohibition against the uncloistered or vagabond religious issued by Boniface VIII, denunciations by bishops and synods, and charges of heresy to discourage the movement or get the women attached to the Dominican order.[43]

Prostitutes likewise came under spatial confinement. The city fathers relegated these independent, single, loose women to houses or quarters so that they could be regulated. In London they were to practice their trade in their stews across the river from the city in Southwark.[44] On the Continent urban centers undertook to run houses of prostitution, and regulate and tax the women. Sometimes these

---

[42] Bolton, "Mulieres Sanctae," 144–51.
[43] McDonnell, *Beguines and Beghards*, 505–33.
[44] Karras, "The Regulation of Brothels in Later Medieval England," 399–433.

houses of prostitution even went by the name of nunneries, but for the most part they were bathhouses.[45]

When women did move out of their space, they had to do so with proper escort or risk humiliation or even rape. The moralist constantly warned that if women went out alone they would lose their honor.[46] Margery Kempe, a bourgeois English woman with a penchant for pilgrimage, feared rape. She did not go on pilgrimages alone but rather in the company of her husband or with companions who made her respectable. Knowing the tabu and risks to women travelling alone, she would not let her daughter-in-law return to Germany alone but rather accompanied her there. Returning to England alone as a matron, she feared that she would be raped along the way. She joined a company going to Aachen and was explicitly asked, "Why, lady, don't you have any man to go with you?"[47] Women who moved out of their space were subject to gang rape in late medieval France, and even the friars seemed, in their sermons against women who wore "lewd" clothing in the streets, to encourage rape as a punishment.[48]

Although medieval society had many ways to define women as respectable matrons or as marginals, one of the simplest but most overlooked by modern historians was the physical boundaries that it erected around women. The space that women could occupy with freedom of movement was the home, the castle, the nunnery, the village, the city quarter. If they moved outside this area, they did so with proper dress, demeanor, and escort, or they risked impingement on their honor or their persons. Spatial confinement was not an unconscious aspect of medieval society but rather a theme that appeared in all types of medieval literature. Once the space of honorable women was defined and its centrality well established, marginal women could be easily defined as those who wandered outside the confines. While I would not argue that women's marginality can be solely defined by the space that they occupied, I am suggesting that space was very gendered in the Middle Ages and that one factor in reaching a definition of marginality for women was gender-prescribed space and the fate of women at its boundaries.

---

[45] See Otis, *Prostitution in Medieval Society* or Rossiaud, *Medieval Prostitution* for examples of work done on medieval prostitution.

[46] Hentsch, *De la littérature didactique*, 132 (*Chevalier de la Tour Landry*, 1346) among others.

[47] *The Book of Margery Kempe*, trans. B. A. Windeatt (Harmondsworth: Penguin, 1985), 271–81.

[48] Roussiaud, *Medieval Prostitution*, 10–26, 151–52.

Ruined Maids: Prostitutes and Servant Girls in Later Medieval England

Ann J. Kettle

> "I wish I had feathers, a fine sweeping gown,
> And a delicate face, and could strut about Town" –
> "My dear – a raw country girl, such as you be,
> Cannot quite expect that. You ain't ruined," said she.
>
> Thomas Hardy, *The Ruined Maid* (1866)

In recent years much popular interest has been shown in three aspects of medieval social history: the history of women, the history of marginal social groups, and the history of sexuality.[1] In the light of recent research in these areas, I intend to examine the evidence for the sexual behavior of two sorts of marginal women, servant girls and prostitutes, in a small English provincial town in the mid-fifteenth century. Although it has been argued that urban life may have offered more opportunities to women in the later Middle Ages than life in the countryside, in reality the majority of women in towns probably led a marginal existence as domestic servants or prostitutes. Recently both these sorts of marginal women have been the subject of research that connects them at various points and both have been subject to feminist interpretations in the areas of sexuality and female independence.

Connections have been made between them in the following ways: both prostitution and domestic service were intermittent, non-productive occupations; both sorts of women were outside family norms and so subject to suspicion and

---

[1] See the following: (on women) Shulamith Shahar, *The Fourth Estate: A History of Women in the Middle Ages* (London: Methuen, 1983); Margaret Wade Labarge, *Women in Medieval Life* (London: Hamish Hamilton, 1986); Bonnie S. Anderson and Judith P. Zinsser, *A History of Their Own: Women in Europe from Prehistory to the Present*, vol. 1 (London: Penguin Books, 1989); (on marginals) Bronislaw Geremek, *The Margins of Society in Late Medieval Paris*, trans. Jean Birrell (Cambridge: Cambridge University Press, 1987); Jeffrey Richards, *Sex, Dissidence and Damnation: Minority Groups in the Middle Ages* (London: Routledge, 1990); (on sexuality) James A. Brundage, *Law, Sex, and Christian Society in Medieval Europe* (Chicago: University of Chicago Press, 1987); *Sexual Practices and the Medieval Church*, ed. Vern L. Bullough and James A. Brundage (Buffalo, New York: Prometheus Books, 1982).

attempts to control their behavior, especially in the area of sexuality; both groups were members of service industries; both occupations mirrored those of respectable women in the provision of sexual and domestic services. It has been argued that at certain times in the later Middle Ages both prostitution and domestic service offered an independence and even modest prosperity to women on the margins of urban society. It has also been claimed that prostitutes were mainly recruited from the ranks of domestic servants. Moreover, there is a contemporary literary connection in that prostitutes and servants were among the groups of women to whom Christine de Pizan offered advice in *The Treasure of the City of Ladies* (1405).

These connections will be explored by an examination of a group of women who existed on the margins of society in the small cathedral city of Lichfield. The history of Lichfield in the Middle Ages is more than usually badly documented, but the chance survival of some visitation material from the mid-fifteenth century makes it possible to investigate the women who were brought to the attention of the ecclesiastical authorities because they were regarded by other members of society as "ill-governed of their bodies." An investigation of the way in which these women were treated should show how much this sort of spotlight can reveal about attitudes to women, sexuality, and marginality in later medieval England.

Female domestic servants were integral to later medieval urban society, but very little is known about their origins, working conditions, and life-cycles. These women formed a significant proportion of the female populations of towns but were marginal in the sense that they have left so few traces of their existence. In the sources in which they do appear, they are often identified only by their christian name and the name of their employer. The work of Jeremy Goldberg on York, using mainly ecclesiastical records, has revealed the distinctive nature of female domestic service.[2] The maidservants were young; usually they were immigrants into the city, unmarried and living in the homes of their employers. They entered into yearly contracts and were mobile in the sense that they usually had several employers before marrying. The shortage of labor after the Black Death offered the opportunity of comparative independence to these young female immigrants. They could acquire useful skills, accumulate their own dowries, and, free from family supervision, conduct their own courtships and enter into late, companionate marriages. This golden age for servant girls was, however, unlikely to have lasted beyond the mid-fifteenth century when deteriorating economic conditions in most towns narrowed the opportunities for female

---

[2] P. J. P. Goldberg, "Female Labour, Service and Marriage in the Late Medieval Urban North," *Northern History,* 22 (1986): 18–26, 35–38; "Women in Fifteenth-Century Town Life," in *Towns and Townspeople in the Fifteenth Century*, ed. John A. F. Thomson (Gloucester: Alan Sutton, 1988), 107, 112–15; "Women's Work, Women's Role in the Late Medieval North," in *Profit, Piety and the Professions in Late Medieval England*, ed. Michael Hicks (Gloucester: Alan Sutton, 1990), 36, 39. See also Maryanne Kowaleski, "Women's Work in a Market Town: Exeter in the Late Fourteenth Century," in *Women and Work in Preindustrial Europe*, ed. Barbara A. Hanawalt (Bloomington: Indiana University Press, 1986), 153–54.

service. From that period there are more examples of young women being forced by poverty into crime and prostitution.

Other research has concentrated on contemporary attitudes to young unmarried women who were outside the established family norms. They were viewed with suspicion, and in some towns they were not allowed to live on their own. In Coventry, for example, young women were ordered in 1495 either to enter domestic service or to take a room with someone respectable who would answer for their good behavior.[3] Even as domestic servants, they could be the cause of sexual tension and were exposed to sexual exploitation by their masters. It has even been argued that a new hagiographic genre of the servant-saint was developed by the church as a means of maintaining the allegiance of this marginal class.[4] Contemporary advice to married women, such as that delivered by Christine de Pizan, stressed the importance of the careful choice and strict supervision of maidservants, the regulation of their behavior and the need to provide them with religious and moral instruction. Christine de Pizan sternly reminded maidservants of the terrible consequences of adultery.[5] Thus any opportunity for independence which domestic service may have offered to young women was limited by the suspicious attitude of the rest of society toward young unmarried women and by the dangers of sexual temptation and exploitation.

There has been much recent research on prostitution in the Middle Ages. Historians of canon law have revealed the ambivalent attitude of the church to prostitution.[6] It was disapproved of in principle but tolerated as a necessary evil, an inevitable social fact. Prostitutes were seen as women acting in accordance with their sexual character and harsh corrective action was reserved for the clients, often clerical, of the prostitutes and for the pimps and procurers who protected and encouraged them and profited from their activities. The attitude of the town authorities was also ambivalent: sometimes the prostitutes were humiliated and expelled; sometimes they were isolated in municipal brothels or exploited by the imposition of heavy fines and rents.

The availability of sources has led to a concentration on the institutionalization of prostitution, especially in some French cities.[7] This approach is not appropriate

[3] *The Coventry Leet Book, or Mayor's Register, Containing Records of the City Court or View of Frankpledge, A.D. 1420–1555, with Divers Other Matters*, ed. Mary D. Harris, EETS OS 134, 135, 138, 146 (London: Kegan Paul, Trench, Trübner & Co., 1907–13), 568.

[4] Michael Goodich, "*Ancilla Dei*: The Servant as Saint in the Late Middle Ages," in *Women in the Medieval World*, ed. Julius Kirshner and Suzanne F. Wemple (Oxford: Basil Blackwell, 1985), 119–21.

[5] Christine de Pizan, *A Medieval Woman's Mirror of Honor*, trans. Charity Cannon Willard (New York: Persea Books, 1989), 211–14.

[6] James A. Brundage, "Prostitution in the Medieval Canon Law," in *Sisters and Workers in the Middle Ages*, ed. Judith M. Bennett, Elizabeth A. Clark, Jean F. O'Barr, B. Anne Vilen, and Sarah Westphal-Wihl (Chicago: University of Chicago Press, 1989), 80, 84–89, 94, 98.

[7] Leah Lydia Otis, "Prostitution and Repentence in Late Medieval Perpignan," in *Women of the Medieval World*, 157; Leah Lydia Otis, *Prostitution in Medieval Society: The History of an Urban Institution in Languedoc* (Chicago: University of Chicago Press, 1985), 1–9, 13, 21, 60; Jacques Rossiaud, *Medieval Prostitution*, trans. Lydia G. Cochrane (Oxford: Basil Blackwell, 1988), 7, 41.

for England where only the Southwark stews on the south bank of the Thames are comparable to the municipal brothels found in France and Germany.[8] Other sources, particularly the records of ecclesiastical and municipal courts, suggest a wider range of activity, from professional prostitutes to women on the economic margins of urban society who supplemented their meager incomes by occasional prostitution.[9]

Attention has been drawn to another contemporary view, that of prostitution as a service industry, a trade like any other to be regulated and its practitioners controlled. This has been seen by some modern scholars as the way in which contemporary thinkers dealt with female sexuality by conveniently tidying it away. Another modern view sees prostitution as the one trade by which women could earn more than men and a trade that could offer opportunities for female entrepreneurship, an alternative occupation for maidservants and a profitable sideline for some married women.[10]

What little is actually known about the origins and living conditions of prostitutes in English towns suggests that the majority of them were poor, unmarried immigrants and that they were driven to prostitution by poverty and destitution. They existed on the fringes of urban society and were associated with petty criminals and other marginal and disruptive elements.[11] Their disorderly behavior was seen as a dangerous example to young girls and an affront to respectable married women. Christine de Pizan, who had a higher opinion of woman's moral nature than male writers, could not understand how prostitutes could "endure such baseness, perpetually living, drinking, and eating among men worse than swine," but she did not shrink from offering them advice. The only hope she could hold out to them was to repent of their way of life and seek some form of employment such as laundress in a large house, which would keep them away from men and the temptation to revert to their former way of life.[12]

I want now to examine these medieval and modern attitudes to prostitutes and servant girls in the context of one late medieval English town. In the fifteenth century, Lichfield was a small provincial town, dominated by an imposing cathedral in a large fortified close.[13] The population of the city was probably a little over 2,000, and there were about 100 inhabitants of the close. The cathedral and its needs loomed large in the economy of a small town that had no industry

---

[8] Ruth Mazo Karras, "The Regulation of Brothels in Later Medieval England," *Signs* 14 (1989): 399–433; reprint in *Sisters and Workers*, 100–34.

[9] See, for example, Goldberg, "Women in Fifteenth-Century Town Life," 118–21; Derek Keene, *Survey of Mediaeval Winchester* (Oxford: Clarendon Press, 1985), 390–92; Kowaleski, 154–58; Gervase Rosser, *Medieval Westminster, 1200–1540* (Oxford: Clarendon Press, 1989), 143–44, 216, 244.

[10] Geremek, 240; Otis, *Prostitution and Medieval Society*, 65–66, 103; Karras, 113, 123–26; Rosser, 143–44.

[11] Goldberg, "Women in Fifteenth-Century Town Life," 119–21; Keene, 390–92; Kowaleski, 154–56.

[12] Christine de Pizan, 215.

[13] For the history of Lichfield, see *Lichfield*, vol. 14 of *The Victoria History of the County of Stafford* (Oxford: Oxford University Press, 1990).

and only localized trade. The close needed supplies of food and drink, and the cathedral attracted many visitors: pilgrims to the shrine of St. Chad and those with business in the church courts. In addition, Lichfield was on the main road from London and Chester, and there were many royal and noble visitors in the later Middle Ages. Travellers needed accommodation and entertainment. A constant stream of visitors and a large body of clergy and their male servants provided ideal opportunities for female service, domestic and sexual.

An analysis of the poll tax return for Lichfield in 1380 reveals a range of traders and artisans, but only butchers, bakers, tailors, and shoemakers occur more than once or twice; the largest groups were the cottagers and laborers. Although the return is not complete, there are eleven percent more women than men listed and twenty-five percent of the women listed are unmarried. There are roughly equal numbers of female domestic servants and unmarried male servants listed, and they form nine percent of the total.[14]

The history of Lichfield in the Middle Ages is remarkably badly documented, partly because of the wholesale destruction of the records of the cathedral in the seventeenth century and partly because the government of the town was divided between several different agencies, for none of which there are many surviving records. Lichfield had been founded in the twelfth century for the profit of the bishop of Coventry and Lichfield, and it remained technically part of the bishop's manor of Longdon until the Reformation. In the fifteenth century, however, the government of the town was shared between the port moot of the borough and the guild of St. Mary and St. John the Baptist. The guild had been founded in the fourteenth century, and its members included not only the inhabitants of Lichfield but also local clergy and neighboring gentry. In ecclesiastical matters, both the clergy of the close and the clergy and laity of the city were subject to the jurisdiction of the dean of the cathedral chapter.

There are occasional presentments of brothel keepers in the surviving manor court rolls and occasional convictions of clergy for fornication with servant girls in the records of the cathedral chapter. The guild was also concerned with the morals of its members; according to its regulations, any brother convicted of adultery or any other abominable crime was to be expelled if he did not reform his ways. It is, however, the chance survival of a volume of visitation *acta* for the dean's peculiar jurisdiction that provides a unique insight into the realities of daily life in Lichfield in the 1460s and into the way in which the dean attempted to supervise the morals of the city. The dean at the time was Thomas Heywood, the most remarkable man to hold the office in the later Middle Ages. Heywood was connected with the cathedral for nearly sixty years, and he was a generous benefactor of the cathedral, the close, and the city, showing a particular concern for the poor of Lichfield.[15]

[14] The return is printed in William Salt Archaeological Society, *Collections for a History of Staffordshire*, 1st ser. 17 (1896): 161–68, 180–81.

[15] Ann J. Kettle, "City and Close: Lichfield in the Century before the Reformation," in *The Church in Pre-Reformation Society*, ed. Caroline M. Barron and Christopher Harper-Bill (Woodbridge, Suffolk: Boydell Press, 1985), 158–69.

The volume records the presentments of offenders made to the dean at his visitations of the city in October 1461, January 1466, and November 1466 as well as proceedings in his court after the visitations.[16] The volume is badly damaged and, like all such records, is very difficult to decipher. The recording of the visitations is uneven – the third is very much fuller than those preceding it – and many of the entries are incomplete. It does, however, throw light on some otherwise very obscure corners of Lichfield society; and because, as is usual with such records, the majority of the cases recorded concern sexual offences, it reveals a great deal about the behavior of women on the fringes of town life and about the attitudes of the rest of society to such women.

The visitations provided a safety valve for the tensions in society. Sworn men, the respectable members of society, "discovered" offenders to the dean street by street. The presentments reflect public opinion, gossip, and indignation at behavior which was regarded as unacceptable. Those who were accused by public fame were given the opportunity to attempt to re-establish their good name by purgation. Most of those who went to purgation had no difficulty in finding enough neighbors to swear that they were innocent, even when their guilt seemed to be clearly established. It has been shown that purgation was not a reliable indication of guilt or innocence but of the way in which those who had been threatened by gossip could restore their public reputation.[17] In his turn, the dean could show his attitude to moral offences by the penances and other penalties that he imposed on those who chose not to go to purgation; he could also choose to follow up some cases brought to his attention and to ignore others.

The poor state of the document and the uneven reporting of the three visitations make a rigorous statistical analysis of its contents impossible.[18] The visitations provide three snapshots, one more complete than the others, of life on the sexual margins of mid-fifteenth-century Lichfield. It is, however, a distorted picture, seen through the eyes of the respectable members of that society. The gaze of the community was penetrating, and the lack of any privacy made it difficult for those who infringed the rules, especially the rules which governed sexual behavior, to escape the prying eyes of their neighbors. Young women, in particular, were kept under close observation. They were evidently seen as frail creatures, at the mercy of their baser instincts, and objects of temptation to men; they needed to be closely controlled by fathers, husbands, or masters. Absent husbands and clandestine visits by other men would be noted, as would swelling waistlines and unexplained absences. Women without men, living on their own or with other women, were

---

[16] Lichfield Joint Record Office, D.30/9/3/1.

[17] On purgation, see Ralph Houlbrooke, *Church Courts and the People during the English Reformation, 1520–1570* (Oxford: Oxford University Press, 1979), 45–47; Richard M. Wunderli, *London Church Courts and Society* (Cambridge, Mass.: Medieval Academy of America, 1981), 40–42.

[18] The following details are taken from Lichfield Joint Record Office, D.30/9/3/1, fols. 2–4 (October 1461 visitation); fols. 15–17 (January 1466 visitation); fols. 19–27 (November 1466 visitation).

objects of suspicion, as were servant girls of whom their masters appeared too fond.

Sometimes neighborly indignation resulted in direct and immediate action. Mariot Irish was taken from Robert Beckett's bed by irate neighbors; she was later sentenced to five beatings, but he was allowed to purge himself by the oaths of six of those neighbors. The unnamed wife of John Norley broke her husband's head in two places when she found him in bed with a girl in one of the town's brothels. More usually, however, disapproval was expressed by the reporting of offenders at the visitation, which provided the community with the opportunity to draw to the attention of the dean behavior that it regarded as unacceptable. It is not surprising that the majority of those presented were men, who were regarded as responsible for their own actions; but since it usually took two to commit a sexual offence, the records of these visitations offer an opportunity to examine the characteristics of the women who were mentioned in connection with sexual offences, as perpetrators, partners, accomplices, or victims.

What was reported was behavior that irritated or outraged people. This need not be sexual: Joan Bryd was presented as a gossip and scandalmonger (*scandalatrix et diffamatrix*) who washed her clothes on feast days and distracted men from their prayers by her chattering in church. The majority of the presentments, however, concerned sexual matters and centered on the relationship of marriage. Open and regular fornication that did not or could not lead to marriage was frowned upon, especially if it resulted in pregnancy. John Wodward was observed to visit Agnes Saddler every day and to lie in her bed at night; John Hichyns was sentenced to five beatings for fornicating continually with Joan Prese as a man with his wife. If a member of the clergy was involved, the girl was left holding the baby, but many other fornicating couples must have been forced into marriage by pregnancy or social pressure. In appropriate cases of open fornication, the dean could use the threat of marriage in an attempt to end irregular unions. Thus William Person and the woman he lived with as his wife were made to promise publicly to marry if they slept together again. Thomas Hull who had seduced no less than three of his mother's servants was made to give up two of them on pain of marrying within a month if he resumed relations with either of them; he had managed to purge himself when charged with impregnating the third girl. No action is recorded in another case of youthful promiscuity. Sampson Pere, who was master of the guild in the early 1480s, was presented for fathering illegitimate children in 1461 and 1466. Although he boasted in 1461 that he did not care how many women he deflowered, it was reported that he had adhered to so many women that he suffered from "a burning in his rod."

Dean Heywood showed himself particularly concerned to protect the marriage bond and to restore the authority of husbands within marriage. He let Thomas Wylson off public penance to avoid recriminations because he had recently married and his wife was not aware of his misbehavior; the sentence of seven beatings on Wylson's heavily pregnant mistress was also commuted, and she was ordered to return to her husband. Ellen Wyddurley caused a scandal by entertaining male visitors during the absences of her husband, but her husband was persuaded to take her back. Married women living apart from their husbands were repeatedly ordered to return to them. Ill treatment was not an acceptable reason for separation: when Helen Hyndman told the dean that she could not live with her husband because he was a dice player and had wasted their goods, Heywood ordered him not to gamble and treat his wife honestly on pain of three beatings. Couples arriving in the city and claiming to be married were ordered to produce proof of their marriage. Bigamy was likely in two such cases, but usually the woman was suspected of running away from her husband with her lover. Henry Halley was cited for adultery when a woman who was living with him as his wife was reclaimed by her husband.

Within marriage, both men and women were expected to confine their sexual activity to the marriage bed, but although suspicious visits by clerics to married women crop up frequently, only shameful breaches of the rules by husbands reached the ears of the dean. John Atkins, a drover, makes several appearances: in 1461 he confessed to adultery with one of his servants, but in 1466 he was presented for ill-treating his wife and spending most of his time with one of his three mistresses. He was sentenced to seven beatings and ordered to treat his wife better. He managed to purge himself on a charge of adultery with a married woman but was told not to visit her again. Another philandering husband, John Holman, was presented in January 1466 for adultery and treating his wife badly by not giving her food and refusing to lie with her at night as he ought. His behavior did not improve and in November he was accused of adultery with Helen Greenlef, a married woman living in his house. His browbeaten wife, whom he was now forcing to work on Sundays, said that she had seen the couple acting suspiciously on the bed but not actually having intercourse. William Walker was accused of even more serious offences. In 1461 he was presented for adultery both with a servant and his stepdaughter, and was even suspected by the neighbors of child abuse, as he made much of a six-year old girl who was living with him; in 1466 he was merely accused of having two women with him at night. No action is recorded against William Couper who was presented for lying in the same bed as his daughter at night. The seriousness of the charges brought against these married men and the fact that they often managed to restore their reputations by compurgation suggest that more routine and furtive cases of adultery might have been ignored.

Those who were suspected of being pimps and procurers were reported to the dean, presumably because they were seen as a threat to family life by tempting daughters, wives, and servant girls into promiscuity. It seems, however, that it was less the open flaunting of their sexuality by prostitutes which drew complaints from neighbors than the nocturnal noise associated with the trade. There are six cases of houses suspected of being brothels because of the noise coming from them in the middle of the night; significantly, five of the houses were those of women. It was said that so much shouting and chattering came from the house of Margaret Throstyll, a prostitute, that her neighbors could get no sleep.

The women who appear in the visitations, 136 in number or roughly one in eighteen of the adult female population, were clearly mostly marginals, existing on the fringes of respectable society. Those who were said to be married, one-fifth of the total, did not conform to the contemporary ideal of the submissive wife. Quite frequently, they are identified by a different surname from that of their husband. Husbands who were not accomplices in crime were often conveniently absent. Matilda Carver, the mistress of a chaplain, had a husband in Lincolnshire. Margery Beamysh's husband was closer at Burton-upon-Trent, but he was said to be too frightened of his wife and her lover to live in Lichfield. Helen Bowyer refused to live with her husband, Thomas Swanne, and he did not dare to go and see her, even though she had carried off his goods, because she threatened that her friends would kill him.

In contrast many of the unmarried women are identified only by their christian names. Apart from the twenty-three servants, ten of whom are identified by their christian name and the name of their employer, only one woman seems to have had a trade, as a seamstress, and even she is further identified by reference to her married sister. Other women seem to have occupational by-names or aliases such as Matilda Mydwyf, Ellen Nurse, or Rose Mustardmaker alias Lawnderer. Some of their surnames may have had sexual connotations, such as Prymrose or Throstyll. The mother of two prostitutes was known as the widow of Greenhill and her daughters as the sisters of Greenhill, and the husband and pimp of another prostitute was called John Holdmystaffe.

If they did not live in the house of their employer, these women seem either to have lived alone or with other women. Such women without husbands were inevitably objects of suspicion, especially if they received male visitors or had children. Ellen Glyn alias Nurse shared a house with Ellen Wygan; each had a child and was "badly defamed." Ellen Glyn, who was nursing the child of a priest and a dead woman, claimed to have a husband, but when pressed for further details, she said that she had heard that he had died in Wales.

Mobility was another characteristic of life on the margins. These women moved around within Lichfield. Alice Welshman who was presented for opening a tavern on Sundays and feast days and consorting with suspect men in the middle of the night had recently moved from St. John Street to Stowe Street. Another woman who had recently moved was allowed to produce three of her six compurgators from the street where she had formerly lived. These women also moved in and out of Lichfield. Sometimes the absence was temporary, usually to give birth to a child. Helen Swanne was believed to have given birth to the child of Roger Hunt, a notorious fornicator, in Leicestershire. Margaret Harrendon had the child of a married servant of the Archdeacon of Coventry in Warwickshire, and Margaret Glover went to Coventry for the birth of her first illegitimate child. Some women just moved on but appear in the visitations because it was suspected that they were still in contact with their lovers. John Nubold, who was given three beatings for adultery with his servant Margaret Wakefield, was reported to be still acting suspiciously with her, even though she had moved to Newcastle-under-Lyme. Robert Coke, the servant of one of the canons of the cathedral, had fathered two sons on Matilda Frend who lived in Yoxall; they would meet in Lichfield in the house of a procuress. One of John Atkins's fancy women (*pulcras mulieres*) was thought to be living in Lancashire or Cheshire when his case was heard in 1466. Thomas Coke, one of the cathedral clergy, was presented in 1461 for adultery with two women. One of them had since married and moved to Coventry or Nuneaton but was still visiting him in the close as before. The other woman was known only as Agnes: she had lived for a while in the house of a notorious pimp but left "in debt to many"; she then stayed for a fortnight with Matilda Andrew before leaving for fear, she claimed, of being cited and moving, with two gallons of ale, into Thomas's chamber in the close.

This mobility and the static nature of the visitation records make it difficult to chart the path to ruin in individual cases, but there are many examples of young women at the various stages of seduction, pregnancy, promiscuity, and prostitution. Young servant girls, often immigrants from the countryside and without the protection of their families, were particularly at risk, and several of the servants who appear in the visitations were probably already on the road to full-time prostitution, especially those who are described as the servants of other women. There is also evidence of what has been called the stealthy fornication of master and servant.[19] Nine of the servant girls mentioned in presentments for adultery had been seduced by their master or the son of their mistress. The transition from servant to mistress was sometimes observed by neighbors. Isabella Prymrose, who with her sister Agnes visited John Atkins regularly in his barn, was said to be very well-dressed, "far above her status as a servant."

Seduction that could not lead to marriage often resulted in illicit pregnancy; between them, twenty-seven of the women had produced thirty-eight illegitimate children. As might be expected, many of the fathers of these bastard children were suspected to be members of the clergy. In one odd case, two women each blamed the other's pregnancy on a friar; both women were excommunicated. The unmarried mother was put under great pressure to name the father of her child, presumably to discover if marriage was possible, and her parents or employer were liable to find themselves accused of encouraging her in her immorality. Margaret Glover refused to reveal the name of the father of her first child; when she became pregnant again, she said she could not identify the father because "so many men had known her." When her mother and father were presented for encouraging her immorality, she accused William Sumner, a chaplain in St. Mary's church, of being the father of both her children. For her shameless behavior, she was sentenced to be beaten around St. Mary's church on the next five Sundays, dressed in a chemise and tunic with a kerchief on her head and a candle in her hand.

Another case, that of Joanna Bulkeley, reveals the role of the procuress in leading girls into prostitution. Joanna, who was living with Katherine Whytaker, confessed to bearing a child by William Fisher, whom she said had tried to bribe her to swear that he was not the father. She said that she had first slept with Fisher on the Saturday before All Saints Day in 1465 and had been taken to him by Joan

---

[19] Goodich, 119.

Wright, "as she says she has done with others." Joan Wright had appeared in the January 1466 visitation as a suspect woman who encouraged immorality, who had a husband who was often absent, and who sent her son to beg in the close. In November 1466 she was presented for keeping a common brothel and herself committing adultery with four named men, with one of whom her husband had caught her in the act.

The procuring of girls for sexual services took a variety of forms. At one extreme was a brothel. Apart from Joan Wright's establishment, only one other brothel is mentioned by name. In November 1466 a tailor, Alexander Wotton, and his wife were excommunicated when they failed to appear to purge themselves on a charge of keeping a brothel. At the other extreme were those, the majority of them women, who were thought to encourage immorality by opening their houses to all comers. In some cases, they may have been running lodging houses, but if adulterous couples were caught in their houses, they could be accused of procuring. Others were specifically charged with harboring prostitutes. Richard Warner is named on two occasions as the pimp of prostitutes, and Cecilia Whyttfall had two women in her house who were common to all, as was Cecilia herself. Joan Hardey, who had once lived with the notorious Roger Hunt and had borne him four children, had two servants in her house next to the fountain in Wade Street who were common to all. Joan Grenesall was alleged to be harboring two women, Margaret and Agnes, who had come from a London brothel, but she claimed that they had moved on to live with other women in the town. Some women, like Juliana Tatlock, were accused of acting as procurers for only one man; others, like Joan Mosse, were presented for encouraging immorality among many women. In some cases prostitution was evidently a family business: the husband of Alice Jamys acted as her pimp. Joanne Coke, who might be the widow of Greenhill whose two daughters were common to all, was sentenced to three beatings for encouraging immorality between her daughters and those who adhered to them. One daughter had had a child by an unknown father; the other daughter had been made pregnant in Southwell and had given birth there. Other prostitutes, such as Margaret Throstyll or Elizabeth Lecche, seem to have operated independently from their own houses.

In the record of the three visitations, nineteen prostitutes can be firmly identified, in that they are described as being common to all. Except in two cases, it is not possible to discover much more about their conditions of work or the nature and extent of their business. Agnes Browne, who was probably responsible for the burning in Sampson Pere's rod, was said to make regular visits to Burton Abbey to copulate with the monks. Cecilia, a single woman, whose landlord's wife acted as her procuress, boasted in November 1466 that during the Duke of Clarence's recent visit to Lichfield she had made six royals (£3) and had been known fourteen times day and night by members of the Duke's household, especially by one Blasby, a yeoman of the Duke's chamber, who had her as often as he pleased. This particular entry is marked in the margin by a pointing finger, as is the account of John Norley's wife breaking his head when she found him in a brothel.

The paucity of evidence for female domestic service in Lichfield means that little light can be thrown on those young women who found that domestic service offered them the opportunity to amass their own dowries, conduct their own courtships, and arrange their own marriages free of family pressures. These women went from the anonymity of domestic service to the anonymity of marriage. The visitations do, however, reveal the dark side of domestic service: seduction, illicit pregnancy, and sexual exploitation. The ruined maids reported to the dean may well have been on their way to professional prostitution via casual fornication and illicit pregnancy.

The presentments reveal little sympathy for the unprotected servant girl who was led into temptation by her employer or a member of the clergy. There was a general suspicion of young unmarried women, and their behavior was evidently subject to close inspection. There were, however, a surprisingly large number of women who were unmarried or separated from their husbands, and many of them seem to have lived alone or in all female households. It is possible that there was some concentration of such women in the poorer parts of the city, but unattached women seem to have been mobile both within and outside Lichfield.

The concentration of clergy in the city and the close and the stream of visitors to Lichfield provided a steady trade for the small group of prostitutes and for those women who sold their bodies on a less regular basis. Dean Heywood was prepared to punish the men and women who harbored and encouraged prostitutes, but he rarely took action against the women themselves. Twenty years later the guild authorities were not to be as tolerant toward those women who were identified as the cause of much petty crime and disorder. In 1486 an ordinance of the guild ruled that prostitutes, defined as "any misruled woman of her body that is called a common sinner with every person that will dispose himself to meddle with such" were to be put on the cuckstool and after being shamed were to leave the city on pain of imprisonment.[20]

While the visitations vividly reveal the social and sexual tensions in a small community, they also seem to confirm indications noticed elsewhere that social attitudes were beginning to harden at this period. What was coming to be advocated was "a sober life of moderate sexual activity within the bonds of marriage." [21] Although the presentments were made by men, there are some signs that women were also anxious to protect their good names and that married women may have been demanding action against those who appeared to have a casual attitude to sexual activity or marriage. There is evidence of indignation at the open flaunting of sexuality. Women whose shameful condition revealed the nature of their misbehavior were harshly treated, particularly when they were unable or unwilling to reveal the name of the father of their child. Couples who were thought not to be married were ordered to provide evidence of their

[20] *The Gild of St. Mary, Lichfield, being Ordinances of the Gild of St. Mary, and Other Documents*, ed. Frederick J. Furnivall, EETS ES 114 (London: Kegan Paul, Trench, Trübner & Co., 1920), 13.

[21] Otis, *Prostitution and Medieval Society*, 108–9.

marriages, and runaway wives were expected to return to their husbands. Adultery was regarded as something to be watched out for and reported, even if those men suspected of this offence against marriage were able to defend themselves against gossip and by compurgation to reintegrate themselves into their neighborhood.

The chance survival of the record of three visitations of an otherwise poorly documented provincial town reveals something of the life of women on the fringes of medieval urban society. At a time when the opportunities for independence open to young unmarried women were narrowing once again, it seems that many women were either choosing to exploit their sexuality or being forced by necessity into prostitution. The barrier between the marginal and the normal world was becoming higher. If life on the margins of society could offer any independence or relative prosperity to women, it must have been very precarious, and it would have lasted only as long as they were able to exploit their own sexuality or that of younger women.

The Merry Widow's Serious Sister: Remarriage in Classical Canon Law

James A. Brundage

I

The death of a husband and father, especially while his children were still small, was a catastrophe that plunged many medieval families into crisis, a disaster from which few households could hope to emerge unimpaired. The widow's rights to her late husband's property were often severely limited: she could well find herself ejected unceremoniously from house and home, abruptly stripped of status and resources almost immediately following her husband's death – indeed, the new widow could count herself lucky if she kept anything more than her clothing and personal adornments.[1] The severe dislocation of the family economy that followed the death of the male head of household made it practically necessary for the majority of medieval widows to remarry and urgent that they do so at the earliest available opportunity, if they were to salvage anything from the wreckage of family life.

The social situation of the medieval widow was apt to be nearly as dangerous and precarious as her economic plight. Medieval communities offered scant support for isolated women who lacked male protectors, save for the few who became nuns. As adult single women in the world, widows were terribly vulnerable to threats against their persons and their children, as well as to their property.[2]

Although speedy remarriage no doubt seemed the obvious solution to many in these circumstances, it was an option not available to every widow and not

---

[1] See, e.g., Michael M. Sheehan, "The Influence of Canon Law on the Property Rights of Married Women in England," *Mediaeval Studies* 25 (1963): 109–24; Philippe de Beaumanoir, *Coutumes de Beauvaisis* 13.442, 456, ed. A. Salmon, 2 vols. (Paris: A. et J. Picard, 1899–1900; reprint, 1970), 1:211, 219; Thomas Izbicki, " 'Ista questio est antiqua': Two Consilia on Widows' Rights," *Bulletin of Medieval Canon Law* n.s. 8 (1978): 47–50.

[2] David Herlihy, "Marriage at Pistoia in the Fifteenth Century," *Bullettino storico pistoiese* 74 (1972): 3–21; "The Medieval Marriage Market," *Medieval and Renaissance Studies* 6 (1974): 3–27; and *Medieval Households* (Cambridge, Mass.: Harvard University Press, 1985), 76, 102–3, 124–25, 135, 154–55; and Barbara A. Hanawalt, *The Ties That Bound: Peasant Families in Medieval England* (New York: Oxford University Press, 1986), 220–26.

necessarily attractive even to those in a position to avail themselves of it. The possibility of remarriage varied enormously, depending upon the wealth, social rank, age, religious disposition, family connections, and physical attractiveness of the woman. Poor, landless, middle-aged women with small children and few political connections stood slim chance of finding new husbands. While women of ample means and secure social position sometimes preferred the legal and personal independence that widowhood conferred, especially when they compared it to the prospect of renewed subjection to a husband's desires and unpredictable whims, that choice was realistic only for the favored few.[3]

Indeed, even a young widow of wealth, social position, charm, and beauty faced serious problems, although her prospects of remarriage were obviously brighter and her options more plentiful than those of her plainer and more disadvantaged sister. Still, even in her comparatively advantageous situation, she faced potential rivalry and jealousy from other members of her deceased husband's family. Her in-laws might well challenge her continued guardianship of her children if she remarried, while the siblings of her late husband often resisted any claims she might advance for a share in the family resources.[4] Further, since such a woman might have potential value on the marriage market, she might well find herself facing the prospect of remarriage to an unwelcome partner, who might himself abduct her by force, or else be forced upon her by others who stood to profit from her plight.[5]

II

Not only did significant numbers of medieval widows find it difficult to remarry, but in addition both social policy and church law posed obstacles that further complicated the situation of those who had the opportunity to do so and wished to avail themselves of it. This paper will examine the ways in which the law of the medieval church affected these serious but common problems, the policies that it applied, and the limitations that it sought to impose upon the remarriage of widows.

Canonists of the classical period (ca. 1140–1375) were heirs to an abundant

---

[3] The right of elite widows to remain single seemed a sufficiently important issue among the wealthy and powerful in England to secure express acknowledgement from King John in Magna Carta, c. 8; William Stubbs, *Select Charters and Other Illustrations of English Constitutional History from the Earliest Times to the Reign of Edward the First*, 7th ed. (Oxford: Clarendon Press, 1890), 298.

[4] Sue Sheridan Walker, "Widow and Ward: The Feudal Law of Child Custody in Medieval England," in *Women in Medieval Society*, ed. Susan Mosher Stuard (Philadelphia: University of Pennsylvania Press, 1976), 159–72.

[5] Sue Sheridan Walker, "Free Consent and Marriage of Feudal Wards in Medieval England," *Journal of Medieval History* 8 (1982): 123–34; James A. Brundage, "Marriage Law in the Latin Kingdom of Jerusalem," in *Outremer: Studies in the History of the Crusading Kingdom of Jerusalem Presented to Joshua Prawer*, ed. B. Z. Kedar, H. E. Mayer, and R. C. Smail (Jerusalem: Yad Izhak Ben–Zvi Institute, 1982), 270–71.

but ambivalent patristic tradition concerning the remarriage of widows. Eminent authorities of impeccable orthodoxy had declared repeatedly that good Christians could both marry and go to heaven, that disparagement of Christian marriage constituted heresy, and that a widow had a perfect right to remarry after the death of her first husband. But other canonical authorities, equally eminent, strongly deprecated remarriage of widows, discouraged them from doing so, hinted pointedly that remarriage signified shameless slavery to the voluptuous enticements of sexual passion, and lauded, sometimes in quite extravagant terms, the virtue of women who spurned remarriage in order to cultivate in widowhood a second career of consecrated chastity.

Those who taught fledgling canon lawyers in university law faculties faced the challenge of making sense out of this intellectual heritage, of finding ways to harmonize the inconsistent viewpoints of earlier authorities and the discrepancies between patristic exhortations and current practice. I propose here to analyze their efforts to grapple with both the practical and theoretical issues involved in the remarriage of widows and the conclusions that eventually emerged from their discussions.

III

It may seem strange, at first glance, that the issue even arose. Had not St. Paul, after all, confronted the remarriage question and answered it plainly? "A woman is bound by law," he had said, "so long as her husband lives; but if her husband dies, she is freed: let her marry whom she will in the Lord" (1 Cor. 7:39).[6] Apostolic authority might seem to have settled the matter once and for all. True, Paul strongly encouraged widows and widowers to remain single after their first spouse's death (1 Cor. 7:40) and dicta that passed under his name could be interpreted to mean that twice-married men thereby became ineligible for the office of bishop, although that was hardly an urgent problem for widows.[7] But in any event the apostle had clearly stated that widows could properly remarry.

Still, strong reservations about the morality of remarriage appeared quite early in the history of Christian doctrine. Tertullian, for example, called the remarriage of widows an obstacle to faith and then, as his views became more extreme, had declared that no Christian could decently remarry, indeed that remarriage was as grave a moral delinquency as fornication, adultery, or murder. Remarriage, according to him, was absolutely forbidden for a Christian man or woman.[8] But

---

[6] Cf. Rom. 7:2. Jesus, when confronted with a related question, however, artfully dodged the issue of remarriage altogether; Mk 12:18–25.

[7] 1 Tim. 3:2; Tit. 1:6. Modern New Testament specialists generally agree that Paul himself wrote neither of these, but they probably originated in his circle and may well have reflected his views.

[8] Tertullian, *Ad uxorem* 1.7.4, ed. A. Kroyman, in *Corpus Christianorum, series Latina* [hereafter CCL] (Turnhout: Brepols, 1953–), 1:381; *De exhortatione castitatis* 9.1 in CCL 2:1027; and *De monogamia* 4.3, 10.7, 15.1, in CCL 2:1233, 1243, 1250.

Tertullian's opinions lay outside the mainstream of early Christian belief and in his later years, when he voiced his harshest denunciations of the twice-married, Tertullian had gone over to the Montanist sect, whose teachings mainline Christians rejected as heretical.[9] Other sectarian groups, moreover, such as the Manichaeans, also condemned remarriage of widows and even excluded remarried persons from communion on the grounds that they were adulterers.[10] But the Manichaeans, too, were heretics.

Conventional Christian authorities in the West had early sought to distance themselves from such views as these. The first general council of the Christian Church explicitly declared that widows and widowers who remarried should be admitted to communion in the church and condemned those who taught otherwise.[11] But at the same time even conventional Christian leaders actively discouraged remarriage.[12] The Council of Laodicaea, for example, cautioned widows and widowers not to remarry hastily and advised them to undertake a strenuous regimen of prayer and fasting before committing themselves to a second marriage.[13] The Second Council of Braga in the sixth century went even further and required those who remarried to do penance for lascivious conduct, a measure reiterated by other councils, then by penitential writers, and in the eleventh century by church reformers.[14] Moreover, since clergymen who married widows, even if they did so prior to ordination, thereby forfeited once and for all their chances of ecclesiastical advancement, this further circumscribed the marriage market available to widows.[15]

The ecclesiastical status of widows thus remained more than a shade ambiguous. Widows who did not remarry often exercised considerable influence in Christian communities and were in a sense assimilated to the clergy. Indeed many leaders of the early church were drawn from the ranks of widowed men and

---

[9] See generally James A. Brundage, *Law, Sex, and Christian Society in Medieval Europe* (Chicago: University of Chicago Press, 1987), 68–69.

[10] Brundage, *Law, Sex, and Christian Society*, 97.

[11] 1 Council of Nicaea (315) c. 8, in *Conciliorum oecumenicorum decreta* [hereafter COD], 2d ed. by Giuseppe Alberigo et al. (Freiburg i/Br.: Herder, 1962), 9. On the far more negative views of remarriage current among Slavic Orthodox churchmen, see Eve Levin, *Sex and Society in the World of the Orthodox Slavs, 900–1700* (Ithaca: Cornell University Press, 1989), 105–14.

[12] Although prominent churchmen over a long period of time certainly discouraged remarriage, as we shall see, I nonetheless have reservations concerning the argument that this policy was predicated primarily or even in significant part upon the hope that widowed men and women would in the end be constrained to leave most or all of their property to the church; see Jack Goody, *The Development of the Family and Marriage in Europe* (Cambridge: Cambridge University Press, 1983), 94–95, 154–56, and passim; but cf. Herlihy, *Medieval Households*, 11–13, and Brundage, *Law, Sex, and Christian Society*, 606–7.

[13] Council of Laodicaea (ca. 360) c. 1, in *Sacrorum conciliorum nova et amplissima collectio*, ed. Giovanni Domenico Mansi, rev. ed., 60 vols. (Paris: H. Welter, 1901–27), 2:564; Brundage, *Law, Sex, and Christian Society*, 98.

[14] 2 Braga (572) c. 26, 80; 2 Seville (619) c. 4, in *Concilios Visigóticos e Hispano-Romanos*, ed. José Vives, España Cristiana, vol. 1 (Barcelona and Madrid: Consejo Superior de Investigaciones Científicos, 1963), 94, 105, 165; Brundage, *Law, Sex, and Christian Society*, 142, 164, 196.

[15] I have dealt with this matter elsewhere in a forthcoming paper entitled "Bigamy, Spiritual and Carnal: A Study in Legal Theology."

women who had chosen not to remarry.[16] But these were not for the most part ordinary widows – they were virtually without exception women of wealth and power, often closely linked to royalty, and while their piety might inspire their humbler sisters, theirs were careers that few could realistically aspire to imitate.

There was also a feeling that remarriage showed disrespect to the memory of the first spouse. For this reason, among others, Roman law had long since forbidden widows to remarry within a year following the deaths of their first husbands, a policy that both Christians and pagans approved.[17] Romans also considered it inappropriate for widows beyond childbearing age to remarry at all,[18] and held that men who had been widowed and then remarried should be ineligible for the more important priestly functions in pagan worship, a view that the Christian establishment began to imitate almost as soon as Constantine assured the church a settled place within the political structure of the Roman Empire.[19]

IV

As medieval canon law began to reach maturity in the mid-twelfth century, canonists remained aware of the reservations concerning the remarriage of the widowed that had been current in late antiquity and felt obliged to take account of both Roman and patristic practices in their treatment of the law of marriage. Gratian, whose *Concordia discordantium canonum*, or *Decretum* (written about 1140), became the fundamental textbook in the canon law faculties of medieval universities, accordingly found it necessary to address these issues. Although he cited one ancient authority of utmost orthodoxy who had maintained that the remarriage of a widow was a type of fornication (albeit an "honest" one),[20] and another who described the remarried widow as not much better than a prostitute,[21] Gratian made it clear that he rejected these unpleasant characterizations. These statements, Gratian maintained, must be understood as rhetorical devices em-

[16] Peter Brown, *The Body and Society: Men, Women and Sexual Renunciation in Early Christianity*, Lectures on the History of Religions, n.s. 13 (New York: Columbia University Press, 1988), 148–50.

[17] Cod. 5.9.1 pr. (380), 5.17.8.4b (449); Dig. 3.2.11.2 (Ulpian). Citations of the texts of the *Corpus iuris civilis* refer throughout to the critical edition by Paul Krueger, Theodor Mommsen, Rudolf Schoell, and Wilhelm Kroll, 3 vols. (Berlin: Weidmann, 1872–95; reprint, 1963–65). References to the civilian *Glossa ordinaria* are to the Iuntas edition (Lyon, 1584). See also Jean Gaudemet, *Le mariage en Occident: Les moeurs et le droit* (Paris: Cerf, 1987), 42.

[18] They could, however, become concubines; Gian Carlo Caselli, "Concubina pro uxore: Osservazioni in merito al C. 17 del primo concilio di Toledo," *Rivista di storia del diritto italiano* 37/38 (1964–65): 165–68.

[19] Marjorie Lightman and William Zeisel, "*Univira*: An Example of Continuity and Change in Roman Society," *Church History* 46 (1977): 19–20.

[20] Gratian, *Decretum* C. 31 q. 1 c. 9, citing St. John Chrysostom; citations throughout to Gratian and other texts of the *Corpus iuris canonici* refer to the standard edition by Emil Friedberg, 2 vols. (Leipzig: B. Tauchnitz, 1879; reprint, Graz: Akademische Druck- u. Verlagsanstalt, 1959).

[21] St. Jerome, cited in C. 31 q. 1 c. 10.

ployed in order to persuade widows to practice continence, rather than as flat condemnations of second and subsequent marriages,[22] and he then cited other authorities who taught that widows had every right to remarry.[23]

Twelfth- and thirteenth-century teachers of canon law, when they dealt with these passages, elaborated on Gratian's reading of the law concerning this matter. Rolandus (fl. ca. 1150), Rufinus (fl. ca. 1130–1192), and the anonymous *Summa Parisiensis* (ca. 1160) recalled that early Christian communities had punished those who married a second time.[24] Rufinus added that remarriage was once considered a great sin,[25] and that third marriages had been forbidden altogether in the primitive church, although this prohibition, he noted, was no longer operative.[26]

Later canonists generally refused to make any distinction between second and subsequent marriages beyond the first. The eminent thirteenth-century authority, Cardinal Hostiensis (ca. 1200–1271), for example, declared that it made no difference in principle how often a widow remarried; she could remarry a thousand times, he declared, and her last marriage would be just as valid and legitimate as her first.[27]

Commentators on Gratian's *Decretum* nevertheless questioned the value of second marriages (to say nothing of further ones) in the scheme of salvation. Both Rufinus and Rolandus agreed, for example, that only first marriages were fully sacramental and that subsequent marriages, although nowadays permitted, were merely tolerated as concessions to human frailty.[28] This position seemed inconsistent with St. Paul's statements (1 Cor. 7:39 and Rom. 7:2), as Johannes Teutonicus (d. 1245/46) briefly noted in his *Ordinary Gloss* (composed ca. 1215) on the *Decretum*, but other commentators largely ignored that difficulty.[29]

---

[22] C. 31 q. 1 d.p.c. 10: "Verum hoc eum ad exhortationem uidualis continentiae, non in condempnationem secundarum et deinceps nuptiarum dixisse, quam multorum auctoritatibus constat licitas esse. . . ."

[23] C. 31 q. 1 c. 11–13.

[24] *Die Summa Magistri Rolandi nachmals Papstes Alexanders III.* to C. 31 q. 1 c. 8, ed. Friedrich Thaner (Innsbruck: Wagner, 1874), 155–56; Rufinus, *Summa decretorum* to C. 31 q. 1 c. 8, ed. Heinrich Singer (Paderborn: F. Schöningh, 1902; reprint, Aalen: Scientia, 1963), 471; *The Summa Parisiensis on the Decretum Gratiani* to C. 31 q. 1 c. 8 v. *De his qui frequenter*, ed. Terence McLaughlin (Toronto: Pontifical Institute of Mediaeval Studies, 1952), 238.

[25] Rufinus, *Summa* to C. 31 q. 1 c. 10 v. *quantum distat in crimine*, ed. Singer, 473.

[26] Rufinus, *Summa* to C. 31 q. 1 c. 11 v. *trigamos*, ed. Singer, 473; likewise Johannes Teutonicus, *Glossa ordinaria* to C. 31 q. 1 c. 11 v. *trigamos*. The *glos. ord.* to the *Decretum* and to other texts in the *Corpus iuris canonici* will be cited throughout from the edition published at Venice in 1605.

[27] Hostiensis, *Summa aurea*, lib. 4, tit. 33, De secundis nuptiis §§1–2, (Lyon: Joannes de Lambray, 1537; reprint, Aalen: Scientia, 1962), fol. 224va–vb. For similar opinions among theologians, see St. Bonaventure, *Commentaria in quatuor libros Sententiarum* 4.42.3.1 in his *Opera omnia* (Quaracchi: Collegium S. Bonaventurae, 1882–), 4:876–77; Pierre de la Palude, *Lucubrationum opus in quartum Sententiarum* 42.3.1 (Salamanca: Andreas a Portonariis, 1552), 436.

[28] Rolandus, *Summa* to C. 31 q. 1 c. 10 v. *esse desistit*, ed. Thaner, 156; and Rufinus, *Summa* to C. 31 q. 1 c. 10 v. *esse desistit*, ed. Singer, 472.

[29] Johannes Teutonicus, *Glossa ordinaria* to C. 31 q. 1 d.p.c. 10 v. *verum*: "Magister hoc capitulum intelligit de secundis nuptiis licitis, sed competentius intelligitur de illicitis, aliter

Gratian's book left certain important aspects of the remarriage of widows unclear and still unresolved. There was, for one thing, the matter of the nuptial blessing. Although canonists generally agreed that a priestly blessing was not required for a valid marriage, nonetheless it had been usual since the fifth century for Christian couples to receive such a benediction when they married for the first time.[30] But it was also common for the blessing to be denied if one of the partners to a marriage had previously been married. Gratian provided no clear legal authority for this practice, much less for the reasoning that supported it. He also neglected to deal with the question of how soon a widow was entitled to remarry after the death of her first husband, nor did he furnish much guidance for resolving the problems that arose if feudal lords or other authority figures forced widows to remarry and imposed limits on their choice of partners when marrying a second time. Both popes and law teachers addressed these difficulties during the second half of the twelfth century and the first half of the thirteenth.

V

Pope Alexander III (1159–1181) confronted the matter of the nuptial blessing in two decretals that were eventually incorporated into the *Gregorian Decretals* or *Liber Extra* (1234), the principal thirteenth-century collection of the post-Gratian canons. The nuptial blessing must not be repeated, Alexander ruled in the decretal *Vir autem*. If one party to a marriage had received the blessing in a previous marriage, then his or her second marriage could not be blessed.[31] Moreover, Alexander held in another decision, reported in the decretal *Capellanum*, that a priest who bestowed the nuptial blessing on a second marriage committed a canonical offence and should be punished: he was to be suspended from all ecclesiastical offices and benefices until he had made satisfaction for this misdeed.[32]

Alexander failed to articulate a rationale for these two decisions and canonists found them difficult to account for. One theological difficulty that underlay both *Capellanum* and *Vir autem* centered around the problematic relationship between the nuptial blessing and the sacrament of marriage.[33] If marriage was a sacrament,

exemplum de Lamech non congrueret; quare tam aspera proponeret Hieronymus, cum auctoritate Apostoli licita sint, non video."

[30] Brundage, *Law, Sex, and Christian Society*, 88; Gaudemet, *Mariage en Occident*, 265–66.

[31] X 4.21.3: "Vir autem vel mulier, ad bigamiam transiens, non debet a presbytero benedici, quia, quum alia vice benedicti sint, eorum benedictio iterari non debet."

[32] X 4.21.1: "Capellanum nihilominus, quem benedictionem cum secunda tibi constiterit celebrasse, ab officio beneficioque suspensum cum literarum tuarum testimonio appellatione cessante ad sedem apostolicam nullatenus destinare postponas."

[33] The belief that marriage was a sacrament, although still debated among theologians, was by Alexander III's day beginning to be generally accepted; see Brundage, *Law, Sex, and Christian Society*, 254, 431–32; Philippe Delhaye, "The Development of the Medieval Church's Teaching on Marriage," *Concilium* 55 (1970): 83–88; Christopher N. L. Brooke, *The Medieval Idea of Marriage* (Oxford: Oxford University Press, 1989), 273–80.

as many by this time believed it was, then was a priestly blessing needed to impart it? If a priest did bless the newly-married couple, did that mean that he thereby became the minister of the sacrament? Or could the couple themselves be said to create a sacramental union through their exchange of consent and their ratification of that consent by sexual consummation? Opinions on these questions varied and authoritative answers were in short supply. Alexander III's decretals did little to resolve the problem; arguably, they even made resolution less easy.

Commentators on both decretals muddied the waters further. Bernard of Parma (d. 1266) in his *Standard Gloss* (or *Glossa ordinaria*) to the *Decretals*, for example, suggested that the reason why it was forbidden to give the nuptial blessing in a second marriage might be that a sacrament could not be repeated.[34] But that reasoning would not work, as Bernard himself acknowledged. For one thing, some sacraments certainly could be received more than once, most obviously the sacraments of penance and the eucharist, and some writers would add extreme unction to the list as well. Bernard was no doubt drawing here upon the comments of Geoffrey of Trani (d. 1245), whose list of sacraments that could be repeated also included ordination and the laying on of hands.[35] Geoffrey had concluded that the prohibition of the nuptial blessing for second marriages must have been intended to encourage widows and widowers to commit themselves to a life of sexual continence when their first spouses died.

Bernard of Parma further noted that identifying the nuptial blessing as the constitutive act in conferring the sacrament of marriage raised difficult problems, both in law and theology. If the nuptial blessing was essential to marriage, then it might seem to follow that Mary and Joseph, the earthly parents of Jesus, had not been married, and that seemed quite an unacceptable consequence.[36] More-

---

[34] Bernard of Parma, *Glos. ord.* to X 4.21.1 v. *cum secunda*: "Secunde nuptie benedicende non sint, infra eodem vir autem [X 4.21.3]; et secundam accipere secundum veritatis rationem, vere fornicatio est, 30 q. 3 hac ratione [*recte*: C. 31 q. 1 c. 9]. Sed illud intelligitur prima viuente, et non debent benedici secunde nuptie ad exhortationem continentie, sic et sacerdos interesse non debet nuptiis clandestine contractis, supra de cland. matrimonio, cum inhibitio § sane [X 4.3.3 §2]; multo minus debet illas benedicere, et alia ratio est quia sacramentum iterari non debet, infra eodem vir autem [X 4.21.3] ubi haec ratio notatur." *Glos. ord.* to X 4.21.3 v. *iterari*: "Sacramenta enim iterari non debent, 1 q. 1 hanc regulam [C. 1 q. 1 c. 57] et c. hi [C. 1 q. 1 c. 51], ne fiat eis iniuria, 1 q. 1 quidam [C. 1 q. 1 d.a.c. 1] et de consecr. dist. 4 ostenditur [D. 4 de cons. c. 32], 33 q. 7 quemadmodum [*recte*: C. 32 q. 7 c. 10], et C. ne sanc. baptiste. 1. 1 et 2 [Cod. 1.6.1–2]. Videretur enim quod sacramentum huiusmodi non fuisset collatum, vel quod inefficax fuisset omnino, et sic fieret iniuria ei, 1 q. 1 sacramenta [C. 1 q. 1 c. 34]. Tamen penitentia bene iteratur, de pen. dist. 3 adhuc instant [D. 3 de pen. c. 32]. Fallit etiam secundum quosdam in extrema vnctione. Quid enim impediret hanc iterari, cum non sit sacramentum, sed oratio super hominem, 1 q. 1 manus [C. 1 q. 1 c. 74], et solemnis penitentia non iteratur, 50 dist. quam his et c. in capite [D. 50 c. 62, 64]. Gratianus tamen dicit quod iteratur secundum consuetudinem quorundam, de pen. distinc. 3 § ex persona [D. 3 de pen. d.p.c. 21], et benedictio ista cum aliquis secundam duxit virginem iteratur secundum consuetudinem quorundam locorum et hoc si Papa sciat talem consuetudinem, alias non licet."

[35] Geoffrey of Trani, *Summa super titulis decretalium* to X 4.21 pr. (Lyon: Roman Morin, 1519; reprint, Aalen: Scientia, 1968), 390–91.

[36] Penny S. Gold, "The Marriage of Mary and Joseph in the Twelfth-Century Ideology of Marriage," in *Sexual Practices and the Medieval Church*, ed. Vern L. Bullough and James A. Brundage (Buffalo, N.Y.: Prometheus, 1982), 102–17.

over, a requirement that marriages be blessed by a priest contradicted other papal pronouncements, including several of Alexander III himself.[37] Beyond that, and even more fundamental, if the nuptial blessing was essential to sacramental marriage and if that blessing could be received only once, it would then follow that second and subsequent marriages were not sacramental marriages, as some commentators on the *Decretum* in fact maintained.[38] Thirteenth-century canonists seemed reluctant to commit themselves on these issues. What Innocent IV (1243–1254) thought about Alexander III's decretals on remarriage, for example, is not clear: he simply passed over *Capellanum* and *Vir autem* in silence when he wrote his massive *Apparatus* on the *Liber Extra*, perhaps because he found them anomalous or difficult to account for. Innocent's contemporary, Cardinal Hostiensis, likewise refrained from committing himself on the relationship between the blessing and the sacrament. In his *Golden Summa*, an early work (completed in 1253), Hostiensis argued that the crucial element in accounting for the ban on repetition of the nuptial blessing might be sexual relations between the couple. To illustrate this point he posed a hypothetical problem. Suppose that a couple, having married and received the nuptial blessing, then divorced before consummating their union. If they subsequently remarried could they receive the nuptial blessing a second time? In his discussion of this problem, Hostiensis made a strong case that they could, but eventually concluded that priests and couples must comply with the ruling in *Vir autem*.[39] He did not, however, deal with the relationship between the nuptial blessing and the sacramental character of marriage. In his *Lectura*, a systematic commentary on the *Gregorian Decretals* finished at the end of his career, Hostiensis merely reported the opinion of others that the prohibition was intended to discourage second marriages.[40]

Thirteenth-century theologians had little more success than the canonists in accounting for the prohibition of the nuptial blessing. St. Bonaventure (ca. 1215–1274), for example, maintained that since the pope forbade the nuptial blessing to be given to second marriages, those marriages were sacramentally incomplete – although he evaded the issue of whether the blessing was an essential constitutive element of marriage or not.[41]

---

[37] Brundage, *Law, Sex, and Christian Society*, 331–37, and "Marriage and Sexuality in the Decretals of Pope Alexander III," in *Miscellanea Rolando Bandinelli Papa Alessandro III*, ed. Filippo Liotta (Siena: Accademia Senese degli Intronati, 1986), 59–83.

[38] See above, n. 33.

[39] Hostiensis, *Summa aurea*, lib. 4, tit. 33, De secundis nuptiis, 1537 ed., fol. 224vb. See also Charles Donahue, Jr.'s detailed analysis of this situation in "The Case of the Man Who Fell into the Tiber: The Roman Law of Marriage at the Time of the Glossators," *American Journal of Legal History* 22 (1978): 1–53.

[40] Hostiensis, *In quinque decretalium libri commentaria [= Lectura]* to X 4.21.1 v. *secunda*, 5 vols. in 2 (Venice: Iuntas, 1581; reprint, Turin: Bottega d'Erasmo, 1965) vol. 4, fol. 48ra: "Magistri tamen dicunt utrumque dictum ad exhortationem castitatis, alias non vident quare haec benedictio iteranda non sit, quia benedictio quae super homines fit non prohibetur iterari, i. q. i. manus [C. 1 q. 1 c. 74]." He added in his remarks on X 4.21.3 v. *benedici* (ibid., fol. 48rb) that the nuptial blessing was treated as quasi-sacramental, but failed to specify just what that meant.

[41] St. Bonaventure, *Comm. to Sent.* 4.42.3.2 in his *Opera omnia*, 4:877–78: "Resp. ad arg.

Thomas Aquinas (1224–1274) adopted a similar approach, but attempted a fuller and more nuanced analysis than Bonaventure provided. A second marriage, Aquinas argued, is sacramentally complete in itself (*in se consideratum*), but is less complete than a first marriage because it is not a unique relationship between one man and one woman, modeled on the relationship of Christ with the church. For this reason, he continued – and here Aquinas introduced a distinction foreign to the canons – the nuptial blessing is forbidden when both parties are marrying for the second time or if a woman marries for a second time. But the blessing may be given if a man is entering a second marriage with a previously unmarried woman.[42] Aquinas grounded this exception on an analogical argument: although Christ had only one church as His spouse, He was betrothed to many persons within that one church. Similarly, Aquinas argued, a man who contracted a second marriage with a virgin was entering a unique relationship with her, and could therefore receive the nuptial blessing a second time; but a woman who had an earlier husband was not contracting a unique relationship when she married a second husband and therefore was ineligible to receive the blessing again.[43] The reasoning here seems murky and does not perhaps represent Aquinas at his most lucid. The analogy between a second human marriage and the union of Christ and the church seems forced and the rationale underlying the distinction between the second marriage of a widower and the second marriage of a widow is not one of his more elegant arguments.

While academic canonists and theologians had the luxury of debating or ignoring these issues in the relative calm of their lecture rooms,[44] priests charged

---

dicendum quod dupliciter est loqui de secundis nuptiis: aut in se, aut in relatione ad primas; si in se, cum sit ibi consensus expressus inter legitimas personas, est utique ibi sacramentum, nec est ibi carnis divisio, sed unio carnis viri et mulieris; si autem loquamur in comparatione ad praecedentes, sic manet in eis sacramenti ratio incompleta propter carnis divisionem, quia in primis carnem suam univit cum uno, in secundis cum alio, et talis divisio tollit de plenitudine significationis."

[42] For a similar practice in Eastern Orthodoxy, see Levin, *Sex and Society*, 108.

[43] St. Thomas Aquinas, *Summa Theologiae*, Supp. q. 63 a. 2 resp. ad 2 in his *Opera omnia, iussu edita Leonis XIII* (Rome: Riccardus Garonus, 1882–), 12/2:129: "Ad secundum dicendum, quod secundum matrimonium, quamvis in se consideratum sit perfectum sacramentum, tamen in ordine ad primum consideratum habet aliquid de defectu sacramenti, quia non habet plenam significationem, cum non sit una unius, sicut est in matrimonio Christi et Ecclesiae. Et ratione hujus defectus benedictio a secundis nuptiis subtrahitur. Sed hoc est intelligendum, quando secundae nuptiae sunt secundae et ex parte viri et ex parte mulieris, vel ex parte mulieris tantum. Si enim virgo contrahat cum viro qui habuit aliam uxorem, nihilominus nuptiae benedicuntur; salvatur enim aliquo modo significatio etiam in ordine ad primas nuptias, quia Christus, etsi unam Ecclesiam sponsam habeat, habet tamen plures personas desponsatas in una Ecclesia. Sed anima non potest esse sponsa alterius quam Christi, quia alias cum daemone fornicatur; nec est ibi matrimonium spirituale. Et propter hoc quando mulier secundo nubit, nuptiae non benedicuntur propter defectum sacramenti." Hostiensis, *Summa aurea*, lib. 4, tit. 33, De secundis nuptiis §3 (1537 ed., fol. 224vb–225ra) also refers to this practice, but describes it as a *consuetudo prava*.

[44] Jurists' treatments of remarriage problems were not wholly theoretical, however: Bulgarus' students found it screamingly hilarious when, on the morning after his marriage to a widow, the master began lecturing on Cod. 3.1.14, which begins "Rem non novam"; Accursius, *Glos. ord.* to Cod. 3.1.14 pr. v. *rem non novam*.

with the cure of souls had to cope with the practical reality that their parishioners often did marry two or three times and that many of them wanted, or even demanded, that their priest bless their most recent union. Since the pope forbade priests to repeat the nuptial blessing and prescribed serious penalties for those who defied the ban, priests needed to find ways to respect the prohibition while still satisfying their parishioners.[45] Many, perhaps even most, seem to have concluded that since the pope was far away and their parishioners were on the doorstep, they could simply ignore the ban and give the blessing despite the prohibition. For this reason the commissions given to papal legates and nuncios regularly included the power to dispense clerics from the irregularity contracted by giving the nuptial blessing at second marriages.[46] Other priests found means of evading the letter of the law while still responding to the needs and wishes of their parishioners: they confected different blessings to replace the forbidden one and recited the new benediction at a different point in the ritual.[47] Thus they could argue, if the question arose, that they were in technical compliance with the papal prohibition, while the couples whom they blessed were presumably satisfied that they were properly married.

VI

The interval that elapsed between the death of one spouse and remarriage to another was a matter of legal concern only when the survivor was a woman. Ancient Roman custom permitted a widower to remarry at any time after the death of his former spouse, but required a widow to wait for a considerable period before remarrying, both out of respect for her first husband and – what particularly concerned lawyers and lawmakers – to avoid uncertainty as to the paternity of a child born after the death of the previous spouse.[48] Postclassical Roman law established one year as the mandatory period of mourning (*tempus lugendi*) and prescribed the decidedly non-trivial penalty of *infamia* for widows who remarried during that time.[49] In his decretal *Super illa*, Pope Alexander III declared that this

---

[45] Local legislation in Spanish councils and synods occasionally specified that the blessing could be repeated if the wife was still a virgin, even though her husband had previously consummated an earlier marriage. Those who took this position sometimes relied upon the authority of Pope John XXII as justification, although that pontiff, too, had confessed some puzzlement about the law on this point; Federico R. Aznar Gil, *La institución matrimonial en la hispania cristiana bajo–medieval (1215–1563)*, Bibliotheca Salmanticensis, Estudios 123 (Salamanca: Publicaciones Universidad Pontificia Salamanca / Caja Salamanca, 1990), 257–58.

[46] G. Mollat, "La bénédiction des secondes noces," in *Études d'histoire de droit canonique dédiées à Gabriel Le Bras*, 2 vols. (Paris: Sirey, 1965), 2:1337–39.

[47] Jean-Baptiste Molin and Protais Mutembe, *Le rituel du mariage en France du XIIe au XVIe siècle*, Théologie historique, vol. 26 (Paris: Beauchesne, 1974), 243–44.

[48] J. A. C. Thomas, *Textbook of Roman Law* (Amsterdam: North-Holland, 1976), 423; Eva Cantarella, *Pandora's Daughters: The Role and Status of Women in Greek and Roman Antiquity*, trans. Maureen B. Fant (Baltimore: Johns Hopkins University Press, 1987), 122.

[49] Cod. 5.9.1 pr. (380), 5.17.8.4b (449). On *infamia*, see generally Peter Landau, *Die Entste-*

restriction no longer applied and abrogated the penalty of *infamia* in these situations.[50] Pope Innocent III (1198–1216) reaffirmed Alexander III's ruling in the decretal *Cum secundum* in 1201.[51] Western canon law thus permitted widows to remarry at any time without suffering *infamia*.[52] Both pontiffs cited in support of their rulings St. Paul's statement "Let her [a widow] marry whom she will in the Lord" (1 Cor. 7:39).

Canonists commented at some length on both *Super illa* and *Cum secundum*, but addressed their remarks principally to the issue of the conflict of jurisdictions raised by papal abrogation of imperial law. Johannes Teutonicus, commenting on *Cum secundum*, read the decretal expansively and maintained that the ruling exempted widows not only from *infamia*, but also from other penalties that civil law visited upon those who married during the mourning period.[53] Both Hostiensis and Innocent IV argued, however, that *Super illa* and *Cum secundum* should be interpreted narrowly: although the two decretals freed widows who remarried within the prescribed period from the penalty of *infamia*, they left intact the other penalties that civil law imposed on women who remarried in haste.[54] Hostiensis noted (perhaps not altogether seriously) that these decretals suggested that widows whose husbands died while away from home might avail themselves of

---

hung *des kanonischen Infamiebegriffs von Gratian bis zur Glossa Ordinaria*, Forschungen zur kirchlichen Rechtsgeschichte und zum Kirchenrecht, vol. 5 (Cologne: H. Böhlau, 1966), and Elisabeth Vodola, *Excommunication in the Middle Ages* (Berkeley and Los Angeles: University of California Press, 1986), 71–81, 124–25.

[50] X 4.21.4.

[51] X 4.21.5.

[52] Byzantine and South Slavic canon law followed the Roman model; Russian canon law did not, and stipulated no mandatory waiting period before remarriage; Levin, *Sex and Society*, 109–10.

[53] Johannes Teutonicus, *Apparatus* to 3 Comp. 4.16. un., v. *iacturam*, ed. Kenneth J. Pennington, Jr., in "A Study of Johannes Teutonicus' Theories of Church Government and of the Relationship between Church and State, with an Edition of His Apparatus to Compilatio Tertia" (Ph.D. diss., Cornell University, 1972), 646.

[54] Innocent IV, *Apparatus toto orbe celebrandus super V libris decretalium* to X 4.21.5 v. *infamia* (Frankfurt a/M: Sigismund Feyerabendt, 1570; reprint, Frankfurt a/M: Minerva, 1968), fol. 485rb: "<Nota> [*ed.*: Non] solum non teneri infamia, sed nec alijs poenis, quae irrogantur, quia nupsit intra tempus luctus. . . . Ratio diuersitatis est, quia poenae impositae nubentibus intra tempus luctus sunt merae poenae, et ideo omnes poenas a legibus propter hoc inflictas, tolli credimus, sicut infamiam, sed poena quae imponitur secundo nubentibus non est mera poena, imo est prouisio illorum, et ideo non tollitur haec poena per canone, sic etiam non credimus tolli poenas impositas illi qui contra proprium iuramentum nubit, recepta tutela filij non reddita ratione, C. ad Tertul. omnem [Cod. 6.56.6], in Authent. de nup. § sin autem tutelis [Nov. 22.40 = Auth. 22.4.1.]." Likewise, Hostiensis, *Lectura* to X 4.21.5 §2 v. *sustinere iacturam* (1581 ed., vol. 4, fol. 48ra–vb): "Hoc notauerunt quidam quod quamuis infamia sit remissa per apostolum, non tamen aliae poenae reales, in quibus punitur haec mulier per leges humanas de quibus no. e.c. proxi. super verbo tempus luctus [*Lectura* to X 4.21.4 §1], dicentes quod haec mulier videtur dehonestasse primum virum et quasi quamdam causam ingratitudinis contra virum praemortuum commississe, ut innuit dictum Auth. de rest. § unum siquidem [Nov. 39.1.1 in C. = Auth. 41.4.6], ideo tanquam ab ingrata res donatae auelluntur, ar. supra de do., propter [X 3.24.10], nec unquam fuit intentio apostoli quod talis poena remitteretur, et si hoc fuisset, non haberet in talibus potestatem, cum iurisdictiones diuisae sint. . . ."

a loophole in the civil law's waiting period: if a woman first learned of her husband's death 364 days after the event, Hostiensis argued, she could, if she pleased, remarry the following day, since a year would then have elapsed between her first husband's death and her second marriage.[55]

Canonists' discussions of the remarriage of widows during the period of mourning were not simply academic speculations. Civil courts in the thirteenth century continued to impose penalties and disabilities on widows who remarried within the prescribed year of mourning, as canonists well knew.[56] The laws of the Latin Kingdom of Jerusalem, for example, mandated a mourning period that must elapse before a widow (but not a widower) could remarry.[57] Similar provisions appeared in civil laws elsewhere.[58] The laws of the Latin Kingdom were peculiar, however, in that they not merely permitted widows to remarry after the mandatory waiting period had elapsed, but positively required them to do so, on pain of forfeiture of their fiefs.[59] The requirement to remarry was also subject to an unusual limitation, for it applied only to widows prior to the age of sixty. Once past their sixtieth year, widows might remarry but could no longer be compelled to do so. The widow who chose not to remarry, however, must promise to remain chaste and undertake not to use her freedom to lead a life of licentious sensuality.[60]

VII

Legal and theological discussions of the remarriage of widows assumed as a matter of course that widows and widowers enjoyed a free choice of whether to remarry or not. For most widows and many widowers the stark realities were entirely different. The social and economic consequences that resulted from the death of a spouse made it practically imperative for the majority of medieval widows to remarry if they could and to do so with all possible speed.

Academic lawyers and their colleagues in theology faculties focused their discussions of remarriage on the continued sexual opportunities it afforded. They also tended, naturally enough, to discuss remarriage in terms of problems that faced members of the more affluent sectors of society – since the well-to-do were, in fact, far more likely than the disadvantaged to seek legal advice and assistance in resolving their problems. How the widowed felt about the sexual implications

[55] Hostiensis, *Lectura* to X 4.21.4 §2, 1581 ed., fol. 48va.

[56] E.g., Hostiensis, *Summa aurea*, lib. 4, tit. 33 De secundis nuptiis §5 (1537 ed., fol. 225rb–va).

[57] *Livre au Roi* 30 and *Assises des bourgeois* 166–67, in *Recueil des historiens des croisades, Lois*, 2 vols. (Paris: Imprimerie royale, 1841–43; hereafter RHC, Lois), 1:626–27 and 2:113–14.

[58] E.g., in Spain, *Las Siete partidas del rey don Alfonso el Sabio, cotejadas con varios codices antiguos por la Real Academia de la Historia*, 4.12.3, 3 vols. (Madrid: Imprenta Real, 1807; reprint, 1972), 3:83.

[59] *Livre au Roi* 30, in RHC, Lois 1:627; and see generally James A. Brundage, "Marriage Law in the Latin Kingdom of Jerusalem," 270–71.

[60] *Livre de Jean d'Ibelin* 228, in RHC, Lois 1:362–64.

of remarriage is not easy to discover. Certainly the urgency and speed with which widows with modest social and economic resources usually remarried strongly suggests that economic necessity, rather than lust or lascivious desire, may have been foremost in the minds of many. Widows, after all, often needed immediate help in order to keep their households intact, particularly if they had young children to care for. Prolonged widowhood was simply not a realistic option for many of them.

The social situation of widows was typically far more precarious than that of widowers. As adult single women, widows were vulnerable to attacks on both their property and their persons that men in a comparable situation had little reason to fear.[61] But widows typically experienced much greater difficulty than widowers in finding second spouses: they remarried less frequently than their male counterparts and the time elapsed between the death of the first spouse and marriage to the second was appreciably greater for women than for men. Widows who held land had notably greater success in finding a second partner than their more impoverished sisters, and this also suggests that economic considerations, rather than sexual opportunities, were the principal driving forces behind many second marriages.[62]

The long history of ecclesiastical ambivalence concerning the remarriage of the widowed suggests that the authorities who made church law and the lawyers who translated it into practice were attempting without great success to accommodate the necessities of economic and social life among the majority of the widowed with the ascetic sexual ideals of the clerical elite. The result was an intellectually untidy patchwork of policies that did little to respond to the needs and problems of most widows. On the one hand, churchmen told widows that they could remarry, but also told them that they should not. Social and economic necessity required most widows to remarry if they could possibly do so, but ecclesiastical authorities refused to bless their marriages. Widows of modest means were best advised not only to remarry, but to do so speedily. But at the same time civil authorities threatened to punish them if they did so within a year, while church officials promised to nullify those civil penalties.

The confusion and distress that resulted from these disjunctions between policy and practice, I submit, served few well and many rather badly. Canon law concerning the remarriage of widows was no exemplar of juristic ingenuity, for it was neither intellectually coherent nor practically effective. Since the law on

---

[61]   Jacques Rossiaud, "Prostitution, Youth, and Society in the Towns of Southeastern France in the Fifteenth Century," in *Deviants and the Abandoned in French Society*, ed. Robert Forster and Orest Ranum, trans. Elborg Forster and Patricia M. Ranum (Baltimore: Johns Hopkins University Press, 1978), 12, 15–17, and *Medieval Prostitution*, trans. Lydia G. Cochrane (Oxford: Basil Blackwell, 1988), 27–30; Natalie Zemon Davis, "The Reasons of Misrule: Youth Groups and Charivaris in Sixteenth-Century France," *Past and Present* 50 (1971): 41–75.

[62]   Herlihy, "Marriage at Pistoia in the Fifteenth Century," 3–21; "The Medieval Marriage Market," 3–27; and *Medieval Households*, 100–3, 124–25, 135, 154–55; Hanawalt, *The Ties That Bound: Peasant Families in Medieval England*, 220–26; Roderick Phillips, *Putting Asunder: A History of Divorce in Western Society* (Cambridge: Cambridge University Press, 1988), 367–69.

this topic so poorly served the needs of those who most sorely required its protection, a great many of the laity and clergy alike seem very sensibly to have ignored it.

VIII

It remains to be said, however, that when it came to matters other than remarriage canonistic treatments of widows' problems were notably more helpful to the bereaved. Canonists were not unaware that widows in their society were frighteningly vulnerable and asserted that the church had a duty to protect and defend them.[63] In principle, at least (although practice was variable), a fraction of the tithes collected in each parish was supposed to be dedicated to relieving the economic distress of widows and orphans.[64] Moreover, the church courts assumed particular responsibility for safeguarding widows from exploitation and oppression.[65] Ecclesiastical courts had a special obligation, according to Johannes Teutonicus, to protect widows,[66] and Cardinal Hostiensis characterized the Courts Christian as a forum of last resort to protect the rights of disadvantaged widows.[67]

In addition clerics with legal training and forensic skills were supposed to make their services available to disadvantaged persons in general and to widows in particular.[68] The prevailing opinion among academic lawyers held that clerical advocates and other legal practitioners should charge no fees for the services they rendered to poor widows, but ought to furnish their help gratuitously as an act of charity. The commentators admonished practitioners that since God had given them the pearl of knowledge, they were bound to contribute their services to deserving widows in compensation for the gifts they received from the Almighty.[69] While this advice was no doubt morally sound, legal practitioners and even a few theologians were aware that in real life it could be implemented only sparingly. Medieval society produced enough widows, orphans, and other worthy candidates for *pro bono* services to consume all the available time of the advocates

---

[63] D. 87 pr., c. 1–2.

[64] C. 12 q. 2 c. 26–27 and 29–30 allocated a quarter of the tithe revenues to care for the needs of the poor, including widows and orphans, while c. 28 directed that a third of this revenue should be used jointly for maintenance of the church fabric and relief of the poor; for further details see Brian Tierney, *Medieval Poor Law: A Sketch of Canonical Theory and Its Application in England* (Berkeley and Los Angeles: University of California Press, 1959), 68–79.

[65] D, 86 c. 26; D. 87 c. 8; D. 88 c. 1.

[66] *Glos. ord.* to D. 87 c. 1 v. *plus tamen* and C. 23 q. 5 c. 23 v. *oppressos.*

[67] *Summa aurea,* lib. 2, tit. De foro competenti §11, ed. cit., fol. 75rb; cf. Johannes Teutonicus, *Glos. ord.* to C. 24 q. 3 c. 21 v. *pauperem*; Bernard of Parma, *Glos. ord.* to X 3.39.4 v. *non permittas* and X 5.40.26 v. *personarum vel rerum,* as well as v. *viduas.*

[68] 3 Lateran Council (1179) c. 12, in COD, 194, and X 1.37.1; note also X 3.50.1.

[69] Raymond of Penyafort, *Summa de penitentia* 2.5.39, ed. Xavier Ochoa and Aloisio Diez, Universa biblioteca iuris, vol. 1, tomus B (Rome: Commentarium pro religiosis, 1976), col. 518; Hostiensis, *Summa aurea,* lib. 1, tit. De postulando §2, ed. cit., fol. 62ra; Jason del Mayno, *Commentaria super titulo de actionibus, § tripli vero* [Inst. 4.6.24], §54 (Lyon: A. Vincent, 1539), fol. 199vb.

who practiced in the courts. "No one," declared Thomas Aquinas, "can help every indigent," and therefore, he continued, "an advocate is not always obliged to furnish assistance to the poor."[70]

IX

The dissonance between canonistic assertion of the church's duty to protect and assist widows through the courts and canonistic reluctance to permit them to remarry seems symptomatic of a basic ambivalence about the institution of marriage. The contrast here constitutes one more example of the medieval church's *odium sexuale*, that peculiar combination of horror and allure, disgust and fascination, aversion and fixation with which the church's intellectual elite regarded sexual relationships. Remarriage furnished a widow in many circumstances with the most readily available and effective remedy for the manifold disadvantages that she faced. Yet despite the fact that remarriage of widows had specifically received the approval of no less an authority than the Apostle Paul, canonists and theologians clearly felt uncomfortable about permitting widows to remarry. They left little doubt that the basis for their ambivalence lay in the fact that marriage implied sex and that remarriage therefore meant almost invariably that a widow might continue to have sexual relations after her first husband's death. As canonists and theologians saw the situation, a widow faced a choice between contracting a new sexual union or abandoning further sexual opportunities by remaining unmarried. They urgently counselled her to forego marriage, for they believed that choosing the asexual life would necessarily improve her spiritual condition. If she made that choice, the church ought to mobilize its resources to protect her. If, instead, she elected to remarry, she forfeited the assistance of the institutional church, since protection of her interests thenceforth became the obligation of her new husband. The canon law concerning the remarriage of widows thus became an instrument for encouraging and fostering the renunciation of sexual pleasure and the affirmation of ascetic values.

Ecclesiastical authorities clearly preferred to regard widowhood as an opportunity rather than a tragedy. They appear to have been considerably less keen to alleviate the plight of the widow than they were to induce her to reject the sordid solaces of marital companionship and conjugal sex. Defenders of the cold and solitary virtues of celibate denial, who were always inclined to trumpet their own moral superiority to the married masses of the laity, exhorted those newly-bereaved widows who could afford it to renounce once and for all the familiar comforts of domestic life and to embrace instead the austere and lonely purity of convent and cloister.

---

[70] Thomas Aquinas, *Summa theologiae* 2–2.71.1.

The Curse of Chastity: The Marginalization of Women in Medieval Art and Medicine*

Laurinda S. Dixon

"Likewise, ye husbands, dwell with them according knowledge, giving honour unto the wife, as unto the weaker vessel. . . ."

I Peter 3:7

The words "weaker vessel" have been used throughout history to describe women, though today the label is used in conversation more or less as a coy archaism recalling such ideal female traits as daintiness, sweetness, shyness, and amiability. Until recently, however, the term "weaker" literally referred to a predisposition to sickness suffered by all women for no other reason than that they were born female, an accident of birth that brought with it automatic physical and mental debility. Medical authority championed the concept of the intrinsically weak, unstable woman from the earliest times until the present day, though interest in the "flawed" female anatomy peaked in the seventeenth century. During this era, Dutch painters invented a new artistic genre subject, the so-called "lovesick maiden" theme, that illustrates the common view of women as congenitally ill.[1]

Seventeenth-century paintings of ailing women, bearing modern titles like "The Doctor's Visit" or "The Lovesick Maiden" are numerous and, with some variations, alike (Fig. 1). All focus upon a woman – often young, pretty, and well-dressed – who appears propped up in a chair, languishing in bed, or falling down in a faint. She is always pale and listless, sometimes staring vacantly ahead

---

*I wish to express my gratitude to Monica H. Green for her generosity and wise counsel on behalf of this study.

[1] The concept of "lovesickness" was not limited to science and medicine but was also part of a pervasive literary tradition in the medieval era and beyond. For a scholarly discussion of melancholia as a medieval chivalric literary conceit, see Mary Frances Wack, *Lovesickness in the Middle Ages: The "Viaticum" and Its Commentaries* (Philadelphia: University of Pennsylvania Press, 1990). For discussions of lovesickness in the Elizabethan era and the works of Shakespeare, see Lawrence Babb, *The Elizabethan Malady: A Study of Melancholia in English Literature from 1580 to 1642* (East Lansing: Michigan State College Press, 1951); Bridget Gellert Lyons, *Voices of Melancholy: Studies in Literary Treatments of Melancholy in Renaissance England* (New York: Barnes and Noble, 1971); and Roy Strong, "The Elizabethan Malady: Melancholy in Elizabethan and Jacobean Portraiture," *Apollo* 49 (1964): 264–69.

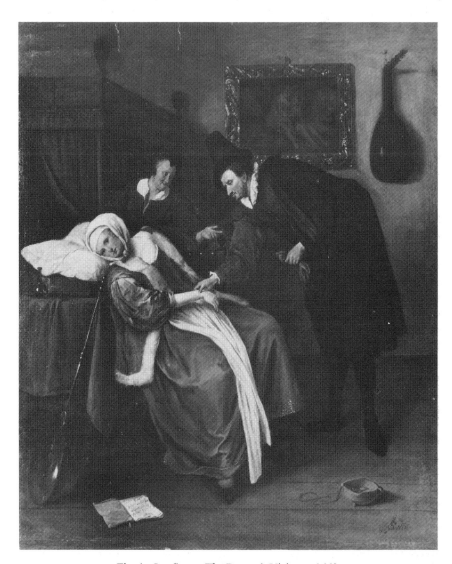

Fig. 1. Jan Steen, The Doctor's Visit, ca. 1663.
The Taft Museum, Cincinnati, Ohio; bequest of
Mr. and Mrs. Charles Phelps Taft.

with sunken, circled eyes or seated in the classic head-on-hand pose of the melancholic. She is usually bundled under several coverlets or wearing a brightly-colored fur-trimmed jacket. Nonetheless, her chemise and corset are often un-laced, revealing a titillating glimpse of ripe bosom and creamy flesh beneath. Despite her state of dishabille, her coldness is emphasized by numerous blankets, charcoal burners, and bed warmers placed about her. Some objects in these paintings are typical accouterments of a seventeenth-century sickroom: bleeding basins, bottles of medicine, urine flasks, and tall straw containers used to contain urine samples when carried to a doctor's office. Other objects, however, are less obviously "medical," at least in the context of our modern sense of what medical is. Often the walls of the sickroom are hung with erotic paintings, or a cupid cavorts atop a doorpost – objects traditionally interpreted as allusions to an absent lover or a case of illicit pregnancy. Usually the woman's doctor attends her, taking her pulse or gazing intently at a sample of urine held up to the light.

The "lovesick maiden" theme has been interpreted variously throughout history, most often as a moralizing sermon against women pregnant outside of marriage, a humorous look at the foibles of young love, or a tongue-in-cheek satire aimed at "quack" doctors.[2] These interpretations, however, reflect a twentieth-century bias. Pre-Enlightenment medicine made no distinction between mental and physical illness, and every fixture of these paintings points to a serious medical concern that involved a large number of physicians in the seventeenth century. It is more logical to surmise that the "lovesick maiden" pictures reflect early theories of gynecology, which assumed a uterine origin for all female illnesses. The specific symptoms depicted in these paintings correspond with a commonly-diagnosed uterine disorder called "hysteria" that was believed to be epidemic among certain types of women throughout the history of medicine.

Like much medical terminology, the word "hysteria," which modern diction-aries define as a psychiatric disorder, is a remnant from the dim past.[3] The word is derived from the Greek word for uterus (*ustera*), and once referred to a plethora of mental and physical symptoms caused by a disorder of the womb.[4] Victims

---

[2] For a sampling of traditional art historical interpretations of the "lovesick maidens," see J. B. Bedaux, "Minnekoorts- zwangerschaps-en doodsverschijnselen op zeventiende-eeuwse schil-derijen," *Antiek* (June-July, 1975): 17–42; Sturla J. Gudlaugsson, *The Comedians in the Work of Jan Steen and Contemporaries*, trans. James Brocknay and Patricia Wardle (Soest: Davaco, 1975); Otto Naumann, *Frans van Mieris the Elder (1635–1681)*, 2 vols. (Doornspijk: Davaco, 1981), 1:102; Einar Petterson, "*Amans Amanti Medicus*: Die Ikonologie des Motivs *Der ärztliche Besuch*," Holländische Genremalerei im 17. Jahrhundert Symposium, Berlin, 1984. *Jahrbuch Preussischer Kulturbesitz* 4 (1987): 193–224; and Peter C. Sutton et al., *Masters of Seventeenth-Century Dutch Genre Painting* (Philadelphia: Philadelphia Museum of Art, 1984), 266, 300, 313.

[3] For the history of the development of the concept of hysteria from its early uterine origin to its acceptance as a psychological condition, see Sander L. Gilman et al., *Hysteria Beyond Freud* (Berkeley and Los Angeles: University of California Press, 1993); and Ilza Veith, *Hysteria: The History of a Disease* (Chicago: University of Chicago Press, 1965). See also the historiographical essay by Mark S. Micale, "Hysteria and Its Historiography: A Review of Past and Present Writings," *History of Science* 27 (1989): 223–61; 319–51.

[4] For discussion of the etymology of the word "hysteria," see Helen King, "Once Upon a Text: Hysteria from Hippocrates," in Gilman, *Hysteria*, 3–90.

suffered apathy, depression, mood swings, perverted appetite, and sleeplessness, accompanied by physical symptoms of listlessness, abdominal pain, difficult breathing, and fainting.[5] As any doctor will tell you, these symptoms have never been unique to women. Pre-Enlightenment medicine did not, however, call men who suffered these problems "hysterical," for they had no wombs. Rather, they were labeled "melancholic." Doctors, quoting Aristotle, believed that melancholia was the privileged complaint of men of genius, and the illness eventually became a mark of gentlemanly privilege among fashionable young men.[6] In women, however, the symptoms of melancholia were believed to be caused by hysteria, a condition in which the womb became inflamed and roamed throughout the body looking for fulfillment – heating and violently compressing vital organs in a "fit" or "paroxysm."

Some authorities denied the possibility of uterine mobility, blaming the symptoms of hysteria upon fumes that originated in the uterus and polluted the body. In order to avoid confusion between the modern psychological condition known as "hysteria" and the "hysteria" of ancient and medieval medicine, this paper will refer to the early uterine prototype of the condition as "uterine suffocation."

Throughout history, the medical establishment has been both awed and threatened by the existence of a unique organ peculiar to women. Most pre-Enlightenment physicians perceived the wayward uterus as an independent animal capable of appetites and movements beyond the control of body or mind. Because all women had wombs, all women were automatically prone to the wayward whims of the beasts within them. For this reason, and because of woman's natural lunar nature, physicians considered the female sex to be innately frail and unstable. Some wondered aloud if women should be classed as human beings or animals. Though all women were endangered by their unpredictable anatomy, women without benefit of marriage – virgins, nuns, and widows – were especially prone to hysteria. Other activities have also been blamed for exacerbating the fickle uterus. Reading too much, working mathematical problems, or engaging in "unfeminine" behavior were activities guaranteed to start the womb on its restless journey. Doctors therefore instructed women that avoidance of matrimony and the pursuance of traditional "male" intellectual activities were against nature and contrary to their best interests. Thus, the sexual subservience of women to men and the lack of support for intellectual accomplishment among women were championed by science, echoed in the dictates of society, and reflected in art.

Art historians traditionally view the "lovesick maiden" theme in Dutch seventeenth-century art as a "new" genre subject filled with moralizing over-

---

[5] For lengthy and detailed descriptions of these symptoms, see Edward Jorden, *A Briefe Discourse of a Disease Called the Suffocation of the Mother* (London: J. Windet, 1603).

[6] The definitive examination of the ancient origins of medical, literary, and artistic images of melancholia is Raymond Klibansky, Erwin Panofsky, and Fritz Saxl, *Saturn and Melancholy: Studies in the History of Natural Philosophy* (New York: Basic Books, 1964). See also Stanley W. Jackson, *Melancholia and Depression: From Hippocratic Times to Modern Times* (New Haven: Yale University Press, 1986).

tones. However, the concept of the ailing woman debilitated by "love" or lack of it is a very old concept that dates far earlier than the seventeenth century. This paper supplies the lovesick maidens with a past, and a venerable one at that. In fact, the earliest extant medical treatises, two Egyptian papyri dating from the second millennium B.C., describe the so-called "wandering womb" syndrome.[7] The Kahun Papyrus (ca. 2000 B.C.) ascribes nearly all pain experienced by women to the womb: "When her eyes ache," it is the "fall of the womb in her eyes," and if her feet bother her, it is also the "falling of the womb."[8] A later papyrus (the Ebers Papyrus, ca. 1550 B.C.) recommends cures designed to lure the uterus back into the abdomen as if it were a living, independent organism. This was accomplished by fumigating the vagina with sweet-smelling vapors to attract the womb back to its proper place, or, conversely, inhaling foul-smelling substances – fumes of wax and hot charcoals – to repel the organ and drive it from the upper body.[9] In addition to being totally autonomous and mobile, the womb was believed to require sustenance in the form of "nourishment," as many of the symptoms suffered by women – depression, hallucinations, and pain in various parts of the body – were ascribed to "starvation" of the organ. Accordingly, Egyptian physicians fumigated the vagina with "dry excrement of men," in an effort to gratify the womb's appetite for sex.[10] The earliest physicians perceived hysteria as an organic ailment and treated the condition with what they considered rational means based upon their observations of the nature of the uterus.

The Egyptian belief in the "wandering womb" was perpetuated by the Greek Hippocratic writers, whose medical works form a corpus that dates from the late fifth or early fourth century B.C.[11] Several of these books, *On the Diseases of Women*, *On Diseases of Young Girls*, and the *Aphorisms*, contain gynecological material. Although these treatises present some inconsistencies, they contain several consistent motifs that would recur throughout the following centuries. One such key concept is the idea of the four bodily humors (sanguine, choleric, melancholic, and phlegmatic) which derive their characters from the four elements (air, fire, earth, and water). Within this system, women were considered

[7] Veith, *Hysteria*, 2–8. For a translation of the Ebers Papyrus, see *The Papyrus Ebers, The Greatest Egyptian Medical Document*, trans. Bendix Ebbell (Copenhagen: Levin & Munksgaard, 1937). For discussion of the gynecological content of Egyptian papyri, see James V. Ricci, *The Genealogy of Gynaecology: History of the Development of Gynaecology Throughout the Ages, 2000 B.C.–1800 A.D.* (Philadelphia: Blakiston, 1950), 12–16; and Henry Ernest Sigerist, *Primitive and Archaic Medicine*, vol. 1 of *A History of Medicine* (New York: Oxford University Press, 1951–61).

[8] Ricci, *Genealogy*, 12–13.

[9] Ricci, *Genealogy*, 16.

[10] See Ebbel, *Papyrus Ebers*.

[11] The relationship between Hippocrates' notion and that of the ancient Egyptians is a point of contention among historians of science who disagree as to whether he had recourse to actual Egyptian sources or arrived at the "wandering womb" theory independently. See King, "Once Upon a Text"; Ann Ellis Hanson, trans., "Hippocrates: 'Diseases of Women I,' " *Signs: Journal of Women and Culture in Society* 1 (1985): 567–82; and Monica H. Green, "The Transmission of Ancient Theories of Female Physiology and Disease Through the Early Middle Ages" (Ph.D. diss., Princeton University, 1985), 13–22.

phlegmatic, their bodies dominated by water. The natural condition of a woman's body was wet, and the lack of moisture upset the balance of humors and adversely affected the uterus.[12]

Hippocratic writers noted that hysteria seemed to occur primarily in older women who, as widows or spinsters, were deprived of sexual intercourse. They concluded that "if women have intercourse, they are more healthy; if they don't they are less healthy. This is because the womb becomes moist in intercourse and not dry: when a womb is drier than it should be, it often suffers violent dislocation." [13] The womb wandered lightly and unimpeded in its search for nourishment, crowding and compressing the other organs. The resulting symptoms varied depending upon the position of the womb within the body. Pressure on the lungs, for example, impeded the flow of air, causing difficult breathing and choking. Should the womb become lodged in the head, the result was pain, drowsiness, and lethargy. Other symptoms ascribed to the wayward womb included fainting, swelled feet, pains in the lower back, grinding of teeth, perverted appetite, and difficulty sleeping.[14] Hippocratic theorists maintained that the womb was better served by wandering to the liver or the lungs, where it could gather moisture from these naturally-wet organs and then comfortably retreat to the abdomen.[15] However, if the uterus remained lodged where it shouldn't be for as long as six months, death was inevitable.[16] Hippocratic cures, like those attempted by the Egyptians, were based upon the erroneous supposition that an unobstructed channel connecting the womb to the head existed within the body. Since the uterus was an independent entity, it could be driven to the nether regions by unpleasant smelling substances placed to the nose or lured back to the abdomen by fragrant douches or fumigations applied to the vagina. Such remedies were effective, but only temporarily. Hippocratic texts strongly recommended marriage as the most effective cure for all single women and condemned virginity as unnatural and dangerous.

Not all ancient medical writers accepted the Hippocratic "wandering womb" theory. The *Gynecology* written by the Roman Soranus of Ephesus (d. A.D. 138) was another important early treatise that would be influential in later centuries. Possessed of a thoroughly independent turn of mind, Soranus rejected the Hippocratic theory of the four humors and denied the supposition that the uterus was capable of movement. He argued that prolonged virginity was actually beneficial to women, who, as a result, were spared from the dangers of childbirth.[17] The Roman Aulus Cornelius Celsus (fl. A.D. 20–30), however, followed

---

[12] Hippocrates, *Des maladies des femmes* in *Oeuvres complètes d'Hippocrate*, trans. Émile Littré (Paris: J. B. Baillière, 1851), vol. 8, bk. 1, par. 7; bk. 101, par. 123–27.

[13] Hippocrates, *Maladies*, vol. 8, bk. 1, par. 7. See also Hanson, "Hippocrates," 583.

[14] Hanson, "Hippocrates," 573.

[15] Hanson, "Hippocrates," 576.

[16] Hanson, "Hippocrates," 574.

[17] Soranus of Ephesus, *Gynecology*, trans. Owsei Temkin (Baltimore: Johns Hopkins University Press, 1956), 40–41. See also the discussion of Soranus' gynecological theories in Green, "Transmission," 23–32.

the Hippocratean format in his "On the Diseases of Women," describing hysteria as a "malignant disease of the womb" and recommending the traditional therapeutical method of luring and repelling the womb by smell.[18] He also advocated exercise and blood-letting, remedies that would become universal in later centuries. A more extensive treatment of female complaints was written by Aretaeus of Cappadocia (ca. A.D. 81–138), who called the contrary womb an "animal within an animal." He described the uterus as "altogether erratic" during its wanderings – capable of violently compressing other organs and even causing death.[19] Despite Soranus' rejection of tradition, the impossibility of the uterus' making an unimpeded voyage throughout the body seems not to have occurred to most ancient Greek and Roman theorists.

The works of Galen of Pergamon (ca. A.D. 129–199) marked the culmination of ancient medicine. Galen, whose writings would dominate medieval and Renaissance medicine, adhered to many Hippocratean beliefs, even while synthesizing and modifying them according to his own vision. He reasoned that the symptoms of hysteria were caused by "repressed semen" and aggravated by sexual abstinence. Galen believed in the existence of both male and female "sperm," and maintained that retention of this substance in both sexes led to corruption of the blood and cooling of the body. The symptoms of hysteria occurred when retained, spoiled spermatic fluid produced noxious fumes that spread throughout the body, disturbing its equilibrium. Thus, Galen opened the door to the existence of male hysteria, though he recognized that the malady occurred particularly among widows, and above all in those who had been fertile and receptive to the advances of their husbands. Galen also denied the theory of uterine migration, cautioning that "we must consider as totally preposterous the opinion of those who, by means of this reasoning, make the womb into an animal." [20] Despite his disbelief in the wandering womb, however, Galen continued to perpetuate the standard Hippocratean odor therapy in which the womb was attracted or repelled according to its own sensory whims.[21]

Recent scholarship convincingly demonstrates medieval gynecological theory derived predominantly from three ancient authors – Hippocrates, Galen, and Soranus.[22] After the fall of Rome, the basis of medical theory, like the Empire

---

[18] *Aul[us] Cor[nelius] Celsus on Medicine, in Eight Books*, ed. L. Targa (London: E. Cox, 1831–36), Vol. 1, ch. iv, 20, 307. See also Heinrich von Staden, "*Apud nos foediora verba*: Celsus' Reluctant Construction of the Female Body," in *Le Latin médical: La constitution d'un langage scientifique. Réalités et langage de la médecine dans le monde romain*, ed. Guy Sabbah, Actes du IIIe Colloque international "Textes médicaux latins antiques" (Saint-Étienne: Université de Saint-Étienne, 1991), 271–96.

[19] (Aretaeus) *The Extant Works of Aretaeus, the Cappadocian*, ed. and trans. Francis Adams (London: Sydenham Society, 1856), bk. 1, ch. 5 and 6; bk. 2, ch. 11.

[20] Galen, *On the Natural Faculties*, trans. Arthur John Brock (New York: G. P. Putnam's Sons, 1916), 44. See the discussion of Galenic gynecology in Green, "Transmission," 36–50.

[21] Galen, *De compositione medicamentorum secundum locos*, ed. and trans. Carl Gottlob Kühn in *Claudii Galeni Opera Omnia*, 20 vols. (Leipzig: Cnobloch, 1821–33; reprint, Hildesheim: Georg Olms, 1965), 13: 320.

[22] Green, "Transmission," cites the influential Hippocratic works: *On the Diseases of Women (De morbis mulierum); Diseases of Young Girls*, and *Aphorisms*.

itself, was split geographically. In the East, Soranus' theories were eclipsed by those of Galen when the ancient traditions became absorbed into Islamic medicine. On the other hand, Western theorists tended to neglect Galen in favor of Soranus, though several Greek texts were translated into Latin and became available to monastic houses. Hippocrates had little direct influence in either the East or West, though his theories showed up frequently as a result of Galen's positive acceptance of the Hippocratic tradition.[23] Until the eleventh century, then, medieval gynecological theory was based entirely on ancient Greek and Roman medical precepts.[24]

Eastern and Western gynecological traditions converged in the southern Italian town of Monte Cassino in the eleventh century. At this time, the drug merchant Constantinus Africanus brought from North Africa several Arabic treatises which had the effect of transforming traditional classical gynecology.[25] What had before been two separate medieval traditions were now fused into something new, as Galenic and Hippocratic theory became synthesized by Arabic medicine. Constantinus Africanus' deed instigated the first sustained effort to create new medical texts and traditions rather than collect and comment upon the old ones. As a result, the medical school at Salerno adopted a gynecology based upon Galenized Arabic theory, spiced with a sprinkling of Hippocrates and synthesized into a Christian matrix. The radical theories of Soranus that had survived in fragmentary form thanks to monastic copiers were largely ignored.

Medieval gynecology was first and foremost a sphere of the male medical establishment which, by this time, was inexorably linked with Christian monastic society. It is not surprising, then, that the misogynist elements of ancient medicine found eager acceptance in this monkish milieu.[26] Perhaps the early Church's persistent distrust of the female sex helps to explain why Galen's fervent denial of uterine mobility seems to have been forgotten by medieval Christian physicians in spite of Galen's pre-eminence in all other aspects of medicine. Instead, gynecological theory championed Hippocratean ideas that tended to reinforce the

---

[23] Hippocrates was translated into Latin as early as the seventh century, and many medieval manuscripts contained condensed passages from the corpus. However, the name "Hippocrates" would not regain its former luster until the corpus was translated from the original Greek in the sixteenth century. See Green, "Transmission," 316; King, "Once Upon a Text;" and George Walter, " 'Peri Gynaikeion A' of the Corpus Hippocraticum in a Mediaeval Translation," *Bulletin of the Institute of the History of Medicine* 3 (1935): 599–606.

[24] The ancients lived on in medical encyclopedias like Oribasius' (326–403) *Iatrikae synagogai* (Medical Collections – a 70-book compilation) and Paul of Aegina's (610–641) *De re medica* in 7 vols. See Green, "Transmission," 77–80.

[25] See Wack, *Lovesickness*, for a scholarly discussion of Constantinus Africanus, a translation of the *Viaticum* and an examination of its various commentaries. See also Karl Sudhoff, "Salerno, Montpellier und Paris um 1200," *Archiv für Geschichte der Medizin* 20 (1928): 51–62.

[26] The literature on the philosophical, religious, and medical justifications for medieval misogyny is vast. Among the works most relevant to this study are Marie-Thérèse D'Alverny, "Comment les théologiens et les philosophes voient la femme," *Cahiers de civilization médiévale* 20 (1977): 105–29; R. Howard Bloch, "Medieval Misogyny," *Representations* 20 (1987): 1–24; Vern L. Bullough, "Medieval Medical and Scientific Views of Women," *Viator* 4 (1973): 485–501; Vern L. Bullough, Brenda Shelton, and Sarah Slavin, *The Subordinated Sex: A History*

debasement of unmarried women by reference to their unstable, "animal" wombs.[27] Such selective theorizing allowed medieval medicine to comfortably combine belief in the uterine origin of hysteria with elements of Christian morality and mysticism. Though Hippocrates was not translated by the Arabs, and his influence was felt mainly by means of secondary references in Galen, the Hippocratean belief in the wandering womb and the dangers of sexual abstinence became hallmarks of medieval gynecological theory.

With Christianity, the popular image of the hysteric changed from a woman beset with physical illness to one at the mercy of supernatural demonic forces.[28] Virgins could tame the heated, bewitched uterus by exorcism consisting of prayer and physical chastisement. A tenth-century Latin document designed for this purpose clearly illustrates the popular Christian belief in the demonic uterus. It is dedicated "To the pain in the womb . . . O womb, womb, womb, cylindrical womb, red womb, white womb, fleshy womb, bleeding womb, large womb, neufredic womb, bloated womb, O demoniacal one!" The invocation that begins the tract firmly melds the image of the wandering uterus with the concept of demonic possession:

> "In the name of God the Father . . . Stop the womb of Thy maid N. and heal its affliction, for it is moving violently.
>
> "I conjure thee, O womb, in the name of the Holy Trinity, to come back to the place from which thou shouldst neither move nor turn away, without further molestation, and to return, without anger, to the place where the Lord has put thee originally.
>
> "I conjure thee, O womb, by the nine choirs of angels and by all the virtues of heaven to return to thy place with every possible gentleness and calm, and not to move or to inflict any molestation on that servant of God, N. . . .
>
> "I conjure thee, O womb, by our Lord Jesus Christ . . . who expelled

---

of Attitudes Toward Women, rev. ed. (Athens, Georgia: University of Georgia Press, 1988), 83–101; Danielle Jacquart and Claude Thomasset, *Sexuality and Medicine in the Middle Ages* (Princeton: Princeton University Press, 1988), 173–77; Aline Rousselle, *Porneia: De la maîtrise du corps à la privation sensorielle, IIe-IVe siècles de l'ère chrétienne* (Paris: Presses Universitaires de France, 1983); and Monica Green, "Constantine Africanus and the Conflict between Religion and Science," in *The Human Embryo: Aristotle and the Arabic and European Traditions*, ed. Gordon R. Dunstan (Exeter: Exeter University Press, 1989), 47–69.

[27] Veith, *Hysteria*, 96. See also Thomas Francis Graham, *Medieval Minds: Mental Health in the Middle Ages* (London: Allen & Unwin, 1967).

[28] The subject of demonic possession and its relationship to female hysteria is a subject of debate among historians. See Jean Céard, "The Devil and Lovesickness: Views of Sixteenth-Century Physicians and Demonologists," in *Eros & Anteros: The Medical Traditions of Love in the Renaissance*, ed. Donald A. Beecher and Massimo Ciavolella (Ottawa: Dovehouse Editions, 1992), 33–48; Gilbert H. Glaser, "Epilepsy, Hysteria and 'Possession': A Historical Essay," *Journal of Nervous and Mental Disease* 166 (April 1978): 268–74; Nicholas P. Spanos and Jack Gottlieb, "Demonic Possession, Mesmerism, and Hysteria: A Social Psychological Perspective on Their Historical Interrelations," *Journal of Abnormal Psychology* 88 (October 1979): 527–46; and Mary Frances Wack, "From Mental Faculties to Magical Philters: The Entry of Magic into Academic Medical Writings on Lovesickness, 13th–17th Centuries," in *Eros & Anteros*, 9–32.

demons . . . not to occupy her head, throat, neck, chest, ears, teeth, eyes, nostrils, shoulderblades, arms, hands, heart, stomach, spleen, kidneys, back, sides, joints, navel, intestines, bladder, thighs, shins, heels, nails, but to lie down quietly in the place which God chose for thee, so that this maid of God N. be restored to health."[29]

The Catholic respect for celibacy presented a medical dilemma regarding hysteria. The Church considered virginity a benefit, not a liability, and prized chastity in women above all other virtues. The ancient view of sex as a natural bodily function unrelated to social stigma or religious morality was in direct opposition to the Christian mandate. Thus, the prized state of chastity could never be thought injurious to a woman's health, nor could sexual intercourse be permitted as a curative measure, for the Church sanctioned the act only as a means of procreation. Sexual pleasure was considered sinful, and erotic urges were believed to be instigated by demons and unholy spirits. The biological inferiority of women made them dangerous to men.[30]

What could a chaste woman do if chants and exhortations failed to budge the bewitched uterus? Such cases demanded the practical knowledge of Galen and Hippocrates which could be found, cloaked in medieval Christian guise, in the gynecological texts produced by the Salerno school. Foremost among these books are the so-called "Trotula" treatises which bear the incipits *Cum auctor* and *Ut de curis*.[31] They were written in the thirteenth century by "Trota" of Salerno, though the adjectival form of the name, "Trotula," is more often used. The authorship of these treatises is a point of debate among historians of medicine; however, the texts themselves claim female authorship and the sex of the author was accepted without question until recent times.[32] The Trotula texts do, in fact, take a generally sympathetic tone which is largely devoid of Christian moralizing. As a result, they were the most widely circulated medical works on gynecology and women's problems from the thirteenth through the fifteenth centuries and, thanks to the invention of printing, remained viable even longer.[33]

The Trotula texts are decidedly Galenic in content and typically Salernitan in their acceptance of the Hippocratean concept of the "wandering womb." Both treatises describe the syndrome, but the less theoretical *Ut de curis* limits

[29] Quoted in Gregory Zilboorg, *A History of Medical Psychology* (New York: Norton, 1941), 131–32.

[30] See Helen Rodnite Lemay, "Some Thirteenth- and Fourteenth-Century Lectures on Female Sexuality," *International Journal of Women's Studies* 1 (1978): 391–400; and, in general, Paul Diepgen, *Frau und Frauenheilkunde in der Kultur des Mittelalters* (Stuttgart: G. Thieme, 1963).

[31] These two treatises are often referred to as "Trotula Major" and "Trotula Minor." A third text, *De ornatu*, also attributed to Trotula, is mainly cosmetic in substance. See the analysis of the two specialized gynecological treatises in Green, "Transmission," 252–314.

[32] See H. P. Bayon, "Trotula and the Ladies of Salerno: A Contribution to the Knowledge of the Transition between Ancient and Mediaevel Physick," *Proceedings of the Royal Society of Medicine* 23 (1940): 471–75; John F. Benton, "Trotula, Women's Problems and the Professionalization of Medicine in the Middle Ages," *Bulletin of the History of Medicine* 59 (1985): 30–53.

[33] M.-R. Hallaert, ed., *The "Sekenesse of wymmen": A Middle English Treatise on Diseases of Women (Yale Medical Library MS. 47, fols. 60–71v)* (Brussels: OMIREL, UFSAL, 1982), 20.

comment to a short passage describing the perils of chastity: "There are certain women who do not engage in carnal commerce, either because of a vow or because they are bound to religion, or because they are widows . . . when they have the desire to have sex but do not do so, they incur grave illness."[34] The *Ut de curis* recommends treating women with a pessary designed to lessen pain, but ignores ancient citations in favor of local Salernitan authors. The more theoretical *Cum auctor*, on the other hand, includes citations to many ancient authors, and devotes much more lengthy comment to the condition of hysteria. Echoing Galen, the *Cum auctor* blames a "superabundance of spoiled seed" as a primary cause of hysteric fits. It notes that "especially does this happen to those who have no husbands, widows in particular and those who previously have been accustomed to make use of carnal intercourse. It also happens in virgins who have come to marriageable years and have not yet husbands for in them abounds the seed which nature wished to draw out by means of the male."[35]

The earliest pictorial ancestor of the seventeenth-century Dutch "lovesick maiden" pictures dates to the time of the Trotula treatises. MS. Ashmole 399, a late thirteenth-century manuscript housed in the Bodleian Library, contains four pages of illustrations unaccompanied by text on both sides of fols. 33 and 34 (Figs. 2–5).[36] Each page contains two miniatures, resulting in eight distinct yet related scenes that comprise the illustrated story. The miniatures themselves are very freely drawn and beautifully colored in light blue and rose pen wash, and are obviously meant to illustrate a case history in narrative form. They are bound among several other texts and illustrations of an obstetrical and gynecological nature, and women are prominently represented in each scene. The subject is therefore assumed to be gynecological, though the folios are inserted not where they would logically belong, among the pages of the *Cum auctor* by Trotula that appears on fols. 21–26, but in a treatise entitled *De stomacho*.[37] In fact, Ashmole

[34] Paris, Bibliothèque Nationale MS. lat. 7056, fols. 8v, 29, quoted by Green, "Transmission," 276.

[35] Trotula of Salerno, *Passionibus mulierum curandorum [The Diseases of Women]*, trans. Elizabeth Mason-Hol (Los Angeles: The Ward Ritchie Press, 1940), 10–11.

[36] Oxford, Bodleian Library, MS. 399, Eng. 1292, fols. 33–34. The manuscript is dated ca. 1292; however, the eight miniatures in question may well have been added in the fourteenth century. See Andrew G. Watson, *Catalogue of Dated and Datable Manuscripts c. 435–1600 in Oxford Libraries*, 2 vols. (Oxford: Clarendon Press, 1984); and Lucy Freeman Sandler, *Gothic Manuscripts, 1285–1385*, 2 vols., vol. 5 of *A Survey of Manuscripts Illuminated in the British Isles*, ed. J. J. G. Alexander (New York: Oxford University Press, 1986).

[37] Other tracts contained in MS. Ashmole 399 include several prescriptions for gynecological conditions dispersed throughout. The most recent identification of the substance of the manuscript is as follows:

fol. 13v:	schematic diagram of female genitalia
fols. 14ra–15ra:	10 fetus-in-utero figures from Muscio, *Gynaecia*
fols. 15rb–16rb:	Constantinus Africanus, *De genitalibus membris*
fols. 18r–21r:	Constantinus Africanus, *De coitu*
fols. 21r–26r:	Trotula, *Cum auctor*
fols. 26r–27r:	Anon. *De spermate*
fols. 26r–31v:	Richardus Anglicus, *De anathomia*

Fig. 2 Oxford, Bodleian Library MS. 399, Eng. 1292, fol. 33r.

Fig. 3 Oxford, Bodleian Library MS. 399, Eng. 1292, fol. 33v.

Fig. 4 Oxford, Bodleian Library MS. 399, Eng. 1292, fol. 34r.

Fig. 5 Oxford, Bodleian Library MS. 399, Eng. 1292, fol. 34v.

399 is a compilation of vaguely related material that could have been bound and
rebound many times within the course of seven centuries. Hence, the placement
of gynecological illustrations within a text dealing with a related organ (i.e. the
stomach) should not be cause for discounting the obvious.[38]

Several historians of medicine and at least one art historian have analyzed the
illustrations in Ashmole 399.[39] They have disagreed not only about subject matter,
but also about the original organization and authorship of the miniatures. The
modern collation of Ashmole 399 begins with fol. 33r (Fig. 2), which illustrates
two scenes identified by Loren MacKinney as "An Ailing Lady" and "Reviving
the Patient Who Has Fainted." MacKinney read the scenes on fol. 33v (Fig. 3)
as "The Patient, Seriously Ill, Undergoes Treatment" and "The Patient Rejects
the Physician's Medicine." He interpreted the two scenes on fol. 34r as "The
Patient Has a Relapse" and "The Patient Has Died: The Autopsy" (Fig. 4).[40] The
art historian Harry Bober believed that fol. 34v (Fig. 5) is in a different hand than
the others, and his opinion is borne out by differences in the style and character
of the drawings compared to the others.[41] Though they may have been added later,
the two miniatures on fol. 34v fit well with the narrative already illustrated in the
previous scenes. MacKinney called them: "Frightened Women Flock to the
Physician" and "The Physician Bids Farewell to Five Well Women."[42] Charles
Singer did not label the illustrations, but it was his opinion that fol. 34, illustrating
the death, autopsy, departing physician, and "frightened women" (which he
called a "consultation"), were originally intended to precede fol. 33.[43] In light
of the art historical opinion of Harry Bober, who believed that the miniatures on
fol. 34v were added to an already-existing group of six, it is logical to accept
MacKinney's rather than Singer's order, beginning with fol. 33r and ending with
fol. 34v. MacKinney saw the eight illustrations as a whole, culminating in a moral
exhortation for women to follow the advice of their doctors, but did not interpret
them in light of gynecological tradition. Singer did not connect the miniatures in
Ashmole 399 as a narrative group, but came closer than MacKinney to giving
them a proper gynecological context. It was Charles H. Talbot who finally
suggested in 1967 that the miniatures directly illustrate the condition of uterine

[38] For discussion of a similarly loosely-combined medical text, containing gynecological
material interspersed with herbal, physiognomic, and astrological treatises, see Hallaert, *"Sekenesse of wymmen,"* 19.

[39] Loren MacKinney, *Medical Illustrations in Medieval Manuscripts* (Berkeley and Los
Angeles: University of California Press, 1965): 100–2; Loren MacKinney and Harry Bober, "A
Thirteenth-Century Medical Case History in Miniatures," *Speculum* 35 (1960): 251–59; Mac-
Kinney and Bober, "La prima autopsia," *Kos* 2 (1984): 51–60; Charles Singer, "Thirteenth-
Century Miniatures Illustrating Medical Practice," *Proceedings of the Royal Society of Medicine*
9, pt. 2, History Section (1915–16): 29–42; and Karl Sudhoff, "Weitere Beiträge zur Geschichte
der Anatomie im Mittelalter, II," *Sudhoffs Archiv für Geschichte der Medizin* 7 (1914): 372–74;
and Charles H. Talbot, *Medicine in Medieval England* (London: Oldebourne, 1967).

[40] MacKinney and Bober, "Thirteenth-Century Medical Case," 251–55.

[41] MacKinney and Bober, "Thirteenth-Century Medical Case," 256–59; MacKinney, *Medical
Illustrations*, 53–56.

[42] MacKinney and Bober, "Thirteenth-Century Medical Case," 255–56.

[43] Singer, "Thirteenth-Century Miniatures," 252.

suffocation described and defined by the Trotulan text that appears elsewhere in the manuscript itself.

The opening scene at the top of fol. 33r (Fig. 2) depicts a woman suddenly seized with the condition who has fallen upon the ground in a swoon, her eyes rolling upward and her arms falling limply at her side. Two alarmed female attendants support her head, while a little dog lies curled at her feet. To the right are a physician, dressed in the academic cowled robe and cap befitting his station, and another figure who appears to be tonsured and who is probably a cleric. Both gesture toward the fainting woman. In this, as in three other scenes, a blank scroll unfurls from the doctor's hand. These scrolls undoubtedly were meant to contain words and captions related to the miniatures. The fact that, in Ashmole 399, they do not suggests that the six miniatures on fols. 33 and 34 were left unfinished. Indeed, there are no scrolls in the last two miniatures on fol. 34v (Fig. 5), which Bober believed were added later.

MacKinney explained the general meaning of this scene as "the lady, seriously ill . . . under the care of a physician."[44] However, several aspects of the illustration allude specifically to uterine suffocation as the condition from which the woman suffers. According to every medical authority, fainting was one of the common symptoms of uterine suffocation or dislocation. Trotula maintained that "Sometimes the womb is choked; sometimes it is lifted upwards . . . sometimes women faint." [45] The artist suggests that the woman's womb has wandered upward by depicting her head as greatly enlarged in comparison not only with the woman's own body, but also with the more natural proportions of the other figures in the scene. Furthermore, the physician clearly points with one hand to the lady's head, possibly indicating the resting place of her errant womb. The pathetic little dog curled up at the woman's feet, its tail between its legs and its tongue hanging out, seems to be suffering in sympathy with its mistress. Singer suggested that the dog is a therapeutic measure, and has been killed to provide medicine for the woman.[46] However, the little dog wears a collar which identifies it as a pet, not a sacrificial victim. The convention of the beloved pet dog mimicking the moods of its mistress is recognized as a common conceit in later art, and perhaps it serves a similar function in this scene.

The miniature at the bottom of the page corresponds distinctly to Trotula's description of uterine seizures and to the therapeutic measure of repelling and attracting the womb by means of smell. It shows an attempt to revive the ailing woman, who now lies contorted upon the ground, completely unconscious. One of two female assistants holds a shallow dish with one hand and applies what appears to be a feather to the woman's nose with the other. The physician stands to the right, accompanied by his clerical attendant, and points with one hand to a glowing fire on the ground before him. The contorted pose of the suffering woman, her legs drawn up to her chest and her arms contracted inward,

[44] MacKinney and Bober, "Thirteenth-Century Medical Case," 252.

[45] Trotula, *Diseases*, 10.

[46] Singer, "Thirteenth-Century Miniatures," 32.

corresponds to Trotula's description of the symptoms of uterine suffocation: "Sometimes the woman is convulsed, her head is brought to her knees, she lacks sight and cannot speak; her nose is twisted, her lips are compressed, she grits her teeth. . . ."[47] Singer quoted a thirteenth-century gynecological passage that describes a similar bodily contortion associated with "suffocacyon of the matrice": "The suffocacyon makyth the matryce [womb] to arise . . . and makyth her to swonne [swoon] and makyth her also to courbe [curve] togedyr her hede and har kneys."[48]

Both Sudhoff and Singer explained the feather placed to the nose of the victim as a method of reviving her and suggest that it has been dipped in an inhalant of oil, water, or vinegar.[49] The feather, however, refers even more specifically to the traditional method of repelling the errant womb by smell. Singer quoted a direct reference to the use of a feather in cases of uterine suffocation: "tak a fethyr [feather] & wet hit in hott water and wete well her face ther with and makyth hote your hondys [hands] and . . . meve [move] ofte her chynne and putte to har nosse thyngys of strong savor . . . at her wyket [wickett, the vulva] lete har tak a fumygacyon of good savour."[50] Likewise, Trotula recommended applying "remedies which have a heavy odor" such as "burnt wool" and "burnt linen cloth" to the nose in order to drive the uterus from the upper body.[51] The effectiveness of this measure was justified by Aretaeus, who maintained that the womb "retreats inwardly if the uterus be made to smell a foetid fumigation, and the woman also attracts it in if she herself smells fragrant odours."[52] Even Soranus of Ephesus, who rejected the concept of the wandering womb, noted that smoldering substances were the most effective in curing uterine disorders, and listed burnt hair, extinguished candles, wool, skins, rags, and squashed bed bugs as substances that emitted especially repellent odors when set on fire.[53] The fire in the miniature and to which the physician knowingly points is therefore an essential component in gynecological odor therapy. The practice of employing fetid, smoky smells to revive a woman who has fainted became standard medical practice for the next millennium. Until the late seventeenth century, this practice was justified by the ancient assertion that the uterus was an independent "animal" with distinct preferences for certain tastes and smells. As late as 1911, long after the stationary uterus had become a fixture of anatomical knowledge, medical handbooks suggested that strong-smelling herbs, called "antihystericals," be

---

[47] Trotula, *Diseases*, 10–11.

[48] Singer, "Thirteenth-Century Miniatures," 36, quoting a paraphrase of Isaac Judeus, an author translated by Constantine Africanus, MS. Douce 37, Western 21, 611, fols. 20r–v (14th century).

[49] Sudhoff, "Weitere Beiträge," 373; Singer, "Thirteenth-Century Miniatures," 34.

[50] Singer, "Thirteenth-Century Miniatures," 36.

[51] Trotula, *Diseases*, 33.

[52] Aretaeus, *Extant Works*, 68.

[53] Soranus, *Gynecology*, 152.

employed to revive women who had swooned.[54] The tradition survives today in the form of "smelling salts."

The top miniature of fol. 33v (Fig. 3) continues the narrative saga of uterine woes. MacKinney labeled the illustration as "The patient, seriously ill, undergoes treatment," while Singer believed that the woman has been taken for dead.[55] Details of the scene confirm both MacKinney's supposition that the miniature is one of a series of events and Singer's belief that it displays the trappings of death. Two crowing roosters perched at the top of the page set the time as the morning of the next day.[56] The woman who, only yesterday, was alive and functioning, lies immobile upon a bier, her eyes sunken deeply into her head. Two funeral candles have been placed beside her, and a vessel of water rests upon her chest. Several friends wearing mournful expressions on their faces cluster at her head while a child kneels at the foot of the bier. The child and two mourners raise their hands imploringly toward the physician who approaches with several attendants and takes the hand of the prone woman in his. Ordinarily, this scene might logically be interpreted as a sad end to the story begun on the other side of the page. However, apparent death was not necessarily the last stage in cases of uterine dislocation. In fact, several treatises describe a death-like swoon that could come over women in the throes of a "fit." Trotula claimed that "the pulse seems to vanish if it is not felt for deeply."[57] Another Salernitan source asserted that "when the breth may not come in ne out the body ys as dede and that ys cause that women otherwhyll [sometimes] by [be] asyounyng [swooning] as they were dede . . . And the suffocacyon makyth the matryce [womb] to arise to the hert & har pulse ys styll." [58] Thus, the physician, knowing the capability of hysteria to simulate death, reaches for the woman's hand in order to "feel deeply" for her pulse. The vessel on the woman's chest would have indicated, by the motion of the water's surface, whether the victim still breathed.[59]

Evidently, the physician was successful in reviving his female patient, for she appears again in the miniature at the bottom of fol. 33v. Here, the woman is accompanied by two attendants, one of whom again holds an object to the nose of her mistress. The physician, now wearing a considerably more placid expression than he did above, stands to one side with his assistant. MacKinney read conflict into this scene, and suggested that the patient has rejected the physician's cure and is throwing away her medicine. He further interpreted the miniature as picturing the angry physician reprimanding his patient.[60] However, assumptions of emotional content in medieval art are always dangerous, as facial expressions

[54] Adolf von Strümpell, *A Text Book of Medicine for Students and Practitioners* (New York: D. Appleton & Co., 1911).

[55] MacKinney and Bober, "Thirteenth-Century Medical Case," 252; Singer, "Thirteenth-Century Miniatures," 32.

[56] I am indebted to Charles Klaus for this observation.

[57] Trotula, *Diseases*, 10.

[58] MS. Douce 37, fol. 20r, quoted by Singer, "Thirteenth-Century Miniatures," 36.

[59] Talbot, *Medieval England*, 81.

[60] MacKinney and Bober, "Thirteenth-Century Medical Case," 253.

and body language were highly codified for representation and can never be interpreted according to modern psychological assumptions. Here again, the pose of the ailing woman, arms hanging limply at her side, legs bent as if to buckle under her, is similar to the pose of the victim in the upper miniature of fol. 33r. This would indicate that the woman is beginning to swoon once again. In fact, she appears to have dropped the book she has been reading and is taking a whiff of another uterine repellent being placed to her nose. Singer believed the object at her nose to be a pin rolled in wool and steeped in aromatic substances.[61] The object could also be a small pharmacists' spatula or spoon upon which some pungent material has been placed. Once again, the ancient Hippocratean odor therapy makes a medieval appearance.

The climax of the gynecological narrative comes on fol. 34r (Fig. 4). The top miniature shows the woman once again in her bed accompanied by three attendants. The physician stands at her feet and has apparently dropped a urine flask that falls upside-down before him, its contents spilling out. Both MacKinney and Singer interpreted this scene as illustrating the approaching death of the patient, perhaps because an autopsy scene shares the page at the bottom.[62] Indeed, hysteria was considered a mortal illness very capable of causing death, especially if uterine fits continued for six months or longer. The autopsy scene at the bottom of fol. 34r has elicited much comment from historians of medicine on account of its unusually realistic depiction of the internal organs. Typical anatomical illustrations of the time tended to present the internal organs according to stereotyped schemata, their shapes and contours regularized and formalized almost beyond recognition.[63] This was especially true of the uterus, which appears simply as a smooth flask with a narrow neck and rounded body on fol. 14r of the same manuscript (Fig. 6). However, this artist evidently had first-hand knowledge of the forms and shapes of the major internal organs. He may even have attended a medical autopsy or anatomy lesson. Whatever the reason for its startling naturalism, this miniature is usually cited as one of the earliest illustrations of anatomical dissection.

The autopsy scene shows the physician and his assistant directing the dissection of the woman's corpse. The knife-wielding subordinate has girded up his robes between his legs so as not to soil them in the dirty task. He has the coarse, slack-jawed face of an illiterate hired hand, and, by all appearances, is not of the same professional class as the university-educated physician who directs him in his task. Singer made much of the difference in appearance between the physician and the dissector, even assuming that the physician is threatening a "low surgeon" who has been "interrupted in his nefarious task" of cutting up a stolen

---

[61] Singer, "Thirteenth-Century Miniatures," 32.

[62] Singer, "Thirteenth-Century Miniatures," 30, 32; MacKinney and Bober, "Thirteenth-Century Medical Case," 253.

[63] See Peter Murray Jones, *Medieval Medical Miniatures* (London: British Library, 1984), 36–55. Typical of the formulaic look of medieval anatomical illustrations is Wellcome MS. 49, fol. 36v.

Si in peđibus ascendit aliquâ parte matris reliquũ corp̃ mclinauerit: qui facere celemus ficut diximus superius obstetrix immissa manu cum componãt. 7 denuç adducat.

Si diuisit peđibus duabus partibus uuluç plantas iunngat quid faciemus immissa manu obstetrix eos iũgat. 7 ad orificium matricis eos componãt. 7 sic adducat.

Si unũ pocem foras biũr q̃ cũq̃ in iudeatur nũq̃ m eū obstetrix teneat. 7 conet ne reliquo corpe infantis plo matre claudat. S: puius infantis digitis ad ungnẽ infantis sint reuocet. immissa manu pedẽ alium colligat. 7 ap̃ sensis pedibus foras adducat.

Si genu ostendat. 7 sic conãt cerre. quid faciemus. retrorsum impelendus est. 7 correctis pedibus est adducendus.

Fig. 6   Oxford, Bodleian Library MS. 399, Eng. 1292, fol. 14r.

corpse.[64] A more likely interpretation was suggested by Karl Sudhoff and championed by MacKinney, that the physician has simply employed a subordinate to
do an autopsy so as to discover the cause of death.[65] This is the more historically
plausible interpretation, as it was common practice for early physicians not
actually to do the dirty work of dissection. Instead, they directed the operation at
a distance, sometimes from a raised platform, and pointed to various organs as
they were revealed by their assistants.[66] The physician pictured here is conforming
to standard medical practice in not performing a "hands-on" autopsy.

The woman's body has been cut open, and all the major internal organs removed
and placed about her. The organs have been identified as the kidneys (appearing
quite oversized) and intestines which appear above the corpse on the picture plane,
and the heart/lungs combination and stomach beneath the body. The dissector
holds the liver, which appears lobed like the hepatica leaf, in his right hand. Singer
and MacKinney, both looking through twentieth-century eyes, believed that the
smooth, elongated form still visible within the body is the spinal column, though
neither the pelvis nor ribs nor any other skeletal formations are visibly attached
to it. Mackinney further identified the curved object just visible between the
corpse's upper ribs as the lower diaphragm.[67] In addition, two modern anatomists
have since questioned the findings of the medical historians, proposing a radically
different interpretation. The woman, they claim, was pregnant and had attempted
an abortion by inserting a mandrake plant in her vagina. According to these
authors, the mandrake caused the woman's death, and the dissector does not hold
the liver, but the plant, which he is showing to the physician.[68] Apart from the fact
that many medieval illustrations of mandrake plants exist, and they look nothing
like the red hepatica-shaped form held by the dissector, such an interpretation
demonstrates how the lack of text in these miniatures inspires specialists from
the historical and clinical branches of the same discipline to arrive at highly
divergent conclusions.[69]

None of the scholars who have lent their expertise and experience to the
analysis of this illustration noticed the most disturbing anomaly in the autopsy

[64] Singer, "Thirteenth-Century Miniatures," 31.

[65] Sudhoff, "Weitere Beiträge," 373; MacKinney and Bober, "Thirteenth-Century Medical
Case," 252.

[66] The most famous illustration of such an autopsy is the "Anatomy Lesson" from Johannes
de Ketham, *Fasciculus Medicinae*, (Venice, 1495). See A. Hyatt Mayor, "Artists as Anatomists,"
Metropolitan Museum of Art Bulletin 22 (1964), 201–20; and Charles Singer, "The Figures of the
Bristol Guy de Chauliac MS. (circa 1430)," *Proceedings of the Royal Society of Medicine*, Section
on the History of Medicine 10 (1917): 73–74.

[67] Singer, "Thirteenth-Century Miniatures," 30; MacKinney and Bober, "Thirteenth-Century
Medical Case," 252.

[68] F. R. Weedon and A. P. Heusner, "A Clinical-Pathological Conference from the Middle
Ages," *The Bulletin of the School of Medicine of the University of North Carolina* 8 (1960): 14–20.

[69] Mandrake plants have distinctive red tomato-like fruit, bushy green leaves, and anthropo-
morphic forked roots. There is nothing represented in the "anatomy lesson" of MS. Ashmole 399
that suggests either the red fruit, green leaves, or forked root of such a plant. For herbal illustrations
of mandrake plants, see Laurinda S. Dixon, "Bosch's 'St. Anthony' Triptych: An Apothecary's
Apotheosis," *Art Journal* 44 (1984): 119–31.

scene. Singularly absent from the array of internal organs surrounding the corpse is the woman's uterus, the one organ peculiar to her sex and which, if we believe the evidence of the five previous miniatures, was the cause of the victim's sorry fate. Where, then, is her womb? It is not possible that the artist purposefully left the uterus out of the autopsy. It is more likely that knowledgeable anatomists have failed to identify it because its appearance in the miniature does not correspond to what we now know to be its proper look and position within the body. The medieval view of the womb's appearance was derived from ancient sources, which described the uterus as shaped like a round bottle with a narrow neck, a form that reflects the characterization of woman herself as the "weaker vessel." This peculiar simile resulted from the belief that the vulva, vagina, and womb of women were not separate anatomical components, but combined in a single, self-contained organ.[70] Anatomists believed that the generative organs of both sexes were the same *in utero*, but that the natural coldness of females hindered their organs from being thrust forward at birth as they were in men, who were naturally warm.[71] Thomas of Salerno's description of the womb affirms this myth: "Its [the womb's] neck is to be compared with the penis, and its internal cavity to the *oschum* or scrotal pouch. The female organ is inverted or turned inward; the male everted or turned outward."[72] The anatomist Mondino de'Luzzi (ca. 1265–1326), though progressive in many of his discoveries, affirmed the standard medieval perception of the uterus, describing it as having "a sort of rotundity and it hath a long neck below."[73] Medieval medical illustrators anatomized the womb accordingly, giving it the appearance of a bottle turned upside-down (Fig. 6). If the miniatures of Ashmole 399 were meant to chronicle a case of uterine dislocation, the womb should appear detached from its moorings and resting in a place where it would not ordinarily be. With this supposition in mind, the smooth white form partially visible between the upper ribs could be seen as the rounded base of the bottle-shaped womb. The long tube-like shape identified by Mac-Kinney as the spinal column would then be the distended vagina from which the uterus has become detached in its journey toward the upper body.[74] Anatomists looking for a recognizable image of uterus, fallopian tubes and ovaries in this autopsy scene would necessarily be disappointed, as this depiction of the female generative organs lacks the realism of the other organs depicted in the miniature. It is likely that the illustrator had never seen a female autopsy, since women were rarely dissected publicly. He therefore would have been forced to rely upon the

[70] For a discussion of uterine pot imagery throughout history, see P. J. Vinken, "Some Observations on the Symbolism of the Broken Pot in Art and Literature," *American Imago* 15 (1958): 149–74.

[71] Hallaert, *"Sekenesse of wymmen,"* 27.

[72] Thomas of Salerno, *Anatomia Vivorum* (13th century), ch. 40, quoted in Ricci, *Genealogy*, 222.

[73] Mondino de'Luzzi (ca. 1265–1326), in Edward Grant, ed., *A Sourcebook in Medieval Science* (Cambridge, Mass.: Harvard University Press, 1974), 733.

[74] Wellcome MS. 49, fol. 38r, illustrates a similar elongated vaginal canal and detachment of vagina and womb. Illustrated in Jones, *Medieval Medical Miniatures*, Plate II.

traditional paradigm of uterine construction in his depiction of the womb. The other internal organs illustrated in the scene are common to both men and women; however, the womb exists only in women. Perhaps in this single instance, the illustrator chose gynecological theory, not anatomical reality, as his guide.

The last two miniatures on fol. 34v (Fig. 5) are a fitting coda to the gyneco-logical narrative. The top illustration shows the seated physician dispensing medical advice to a group of women. A fifth figure, partially cut off at the left margin, holds what appears to be a purse and smiles broadly showing the teeth, an unusual facial expression in medieval art. Sudhoff believed the scene depicts the noble husband of the deceased lady, receiving from her friends a casket containing her heart.[75] Singer identified the smiling figure as the physician's assistant holding a purse in which he collects his master's fees. MacKinney called the upper scene "Frightened Women Flock to the Physician" and interpreted it as a portrayal of the effect of the lady's death on other women who decide to invoke the physician's aid. He suggested that the smiling figure is female, and that her purse-like bag is a pharmaceutical packet containing medicine.[76] If this is the case, all of the figures lined up before the physician are women seeking his advice. The first woman points to her head as the source of her trouble, the next points to her eyes, the third holds a small medicine bottle, the fourth places her hand to her face and vomits, while the fifth holds a medicine bag. All five women appear again in the bottom miniature, bidding farewell to the physician as he rides away on horseback. He raises his finger and looks over his shoulder, as if to admonish his flock not to court medical disaster by refusing the time-honored dictums of the medical establishment.

The eight miniatures of Ashmole 399 illustrate the story of a woman driven to illness and finally to death by the inescapable reality of her sex. The subliminal message, however, is more subtle and was aimed at both physicians and their female patients. The concept of the dangerously fickle uterus, which could be tamed only by the appeasement of its appetites, reflected the common belief that women were predisposed to congenital weakness and ill-health from the moment of birth. Their natural fragility could be exasperated by behavior that deviated from the feminine norm, such as avoiding marriage or over-zealous study. The selective reinterpretation of ancient gynecology within a Christian matrix empha-sized marriage and motherhood as socially-mandated ways for women to attain and maintain their health. The traditional Marian virtues of humility, docility and sexual subservience embodied in the institution of marriage could therefore be seen as both pleasing to men and good for women. Women were effectively barred from traditional male intellectual pursuits and relegated to the domestic sphere. The message expressed in Ashmole 399 is therefore as much moral as medical.

The idea of the wandering womb continued to be a medical mainstay through-out the Renaissance and even gained in strength with new translations of ancient

---

[75] Sudhoff, "Weitere Beiträge," 374.
[76] MacKinney and Bober, "Thirteenth-Century Medical Case," 255.

medical treatises.[77] By the seventeenth century, when the "lovesick maiden" theme in art came into vogue, hysteria was accepted as a disease common to all of the female sex, though this concept was not universally shared by ancient authority. Hippocrates, for example, viewed hysteria as an illness primarily of widows and older women, whereas Aretaeus after him claimed that only maidens were afflicted.[78] The concept of the innate vulnerability of all women did, however, ideally suit the aims of those who opposed post-Elizabethan feminism in the seventeenth century.[79]

The idea of the womb driven to distraction because of unnatural celibacy reinforced the perception of marriage as a socially-mandated way for women to attain and maintain health. In a larger sense, images of ailing women throughout history reveal how the predominantly male medical establishment viewed the female sex and how this view affected society's sense of women's roles and capabilities. Medical tradition held fast to the belief in a mobile, animal uterus which could rise up or send its poisonous vapors forth at any time to destroy the mental and physical equilibrium of the most virtuous, intelligent woman. Though all women were marginalized by virtue of their female anatomy, those without benefit of marriage were more likely to succumb. Belief that women could become sick or even die as punishment for relinquishing their sexual and reproductive roles seems to have been prevalent during times when the dictates of society tended to sponsor a passive, homebound image of womanhood. This image was especially pervasive in seventeenth-century Holland, at a time when feminist consciousness was revived during the years following the successful reigns of several important female monarchs.[80] The argument against female anatomy was again revived during the Enlightenment, when reasons had to be found to exclude women from the new community of free and equal citizens of the world. The nineteenth century held fast to the ancient concept of the unstable womb in order to argue against giving women the vote. Could we, in the twentieth

[77] For a comprehensive study of uterine hysteria as a subject for artists in the renaissance and baroque eras, see Laurinda S. Dixon, *Perilous Chastity: Women and Illness in Pre-Enlightenment Art and Medicine* (Ithaca: Cornell University Press, 1995)

[78] Hippocrates, *Maladies*, vol. 8, bk. 1, par. 7, 32; Aretaeus, *Extant Works*, bk. 1, ch. 5 and 6.

[79] The situation of seventeenth-century women is the subject of many fine studies. A selective list includes Dorothy Anne Liot Backer, *Precious Women* (New York: Basic Books, 1974); Renate Bridenthal and Claudia Koonz, eds., *Becoming Visible: Women in European History* (Boston: Houghton & Mifflin, 1977); Alice Clark, *Working Life of Women in the Seventeenth Century* (London: Cass, 1968); Pearl Hogrefe, *Tudor Women: Commoners and Queens* (Ames: Iowa State University Press, 1975); Rosalind K. Marshall, *Virgins and Viragos: A History of Women in Scotland from 1080 to 1980* (London: Collins, 1983); and Linda Woodbridge, *Women and the English Renaissance: Literature and the Nature of Womankind, 1540–1620* (Urbana: University of Illinois Press, 1986).

[80] The homebound image of Dutch seventeenth-century women is the subject of several recent studies. See especially Wayne E. Franits, *Paragons of Virtue: Women and Domesticity in Seventeenth-Century Dutch Art* (Cambridge: Cambridge University Press, 1993); E. de Jongh, *Portretten van echt en trouw; huwelijk en gezin in de Nederlandse kunst van de zeventiende eeuw* (Zwolle: Waanders, 1986); and Simon Schama, *The Embarrassment of Riches: An Interpretation of Dutch Culture in the Golden Age* (New York: Knopf, 1987).

century, also be marginalizing women by naming Pre-Menstrual Syndrome as the universal debilitating scourge of the female sex? Perhaps if the women who populate the paintings and medical treatises of the past could speak, they would argue against the image of woman as the "weaker vessel."

Maiden Warriors and Other Sons

Carol J. Clover

> Et ne quis hunc bellis sexum insudasse miretur, quaedam de talium femi-
> narum condicione et moribus compendio modicae digressionis expediam.
> Fuere quondam apud Danos feminae, quae formam suam in virilem habi-
> tum convertentes omnia paene temporum momenta ad excolendam mili-
> tiam conferebant, ne virtutis nervos luxuriae contagione hebetari
> paterentur. Siquidem delicatum vivendi genus perosae corpus animumque
> patientia ac labore durare solebant totamque feminae levitatis mollitiem
> abdicantes muliebre ingenium virili uti saevitia cogebant. Sed et tanta cura
> rei militaris notitiam captabant, ut feminas exuisse quivis putaret.
> Praecipue vero, quibus aut ingenii vigor aut decora corporum proceritas
> erat, id vitae genus incedere consueverant. Hae ergo, perinde ac nativae
> condicionis immemores rigoremque blanditiis anteferentes, bella pro basiis
> intentabant sanguinemque, non oscula delibantes armorum potius quam
> amorum officia frequentabant manusque, quas in telas aptare debuerant,
> telorum obsequiis exhibebant, ut iam non lecto, sed leto studentes spiculis
> appeterent, quos mulcere specie potuissent.
>
> Saxo Grammaticus, *Gesta Danorum*[1]

Legends of militant women crop up here and there in Germanic literature, above
all Old Norse. Like their cousins the Greek amazons, the "shield maidens" of
the North have been consigned, by literary historians, to the realm of literary
fantasy. Creatures of the imagination they may be, at least in the form they have
come down to us (mostly in the historically unreliable *fornaldarsögur* and the
equivalent stories of Saxo); but that should not mean, as for the most part it has
meant in Old Norse literary criticism, that they are therefore beyond discussion.
On the contrary, a collective fantasy has much to tell us about the underlying
tensions of the society that produced it; and when the subject is one such as
women, which the "legitimate" sources treat only scantily, the literary fantasy
takes on a special importance. Medieval literature is, after all, rich in transvestite

---

[1] *Saxonis Gesta Danorum*, ed. C. Knabe and Paul Herrmann, rev. Jørgen Olrik and H. Raeder
(Copenhagen: Levin and Munksgaard, 1931), 7:6. Hereafter cited as Saxo. "In case anyone is
marvelling that this sex should have sweated in warfare, let me digress briefly to explain the
character and behavior of such females. There were once women in Denmark who dressed

traditions in both the religious and the secular spheres (e.g., female monks, amazons, *viragines*, Joan of Arc),[2] and one need not look very far or deep to see that the shield maiden stories of the North share with other "women-on-top" traditions (as Natalie Davis has termed them) an underlying concern with the basic issue of where one sex stops and the other begins – not only psychosexually, but also socially.[3] In the case of a certain set of shield-maiden stories we can go even further, for an analysis of their causal logic first in a cross-cultural and then in a legal context leads us beyond a general insight into the Norse sense of sexual borders to a specific insight into the particular role of certain women in the early Scandinavian world of bloodfeud.

Maiden warriors

The story-type I have in mind is that of the maiden warrior: "maiden" because she is usually young and either repudiates or defers or enters reluctantly into marriage, and "warrior" because at least for a time she dresses and arms herself as a man and enrolls in the martial life.[4] The most dramatic of the maiden-warrior

themselves to look like men and spent almost every minute cultivating soldiers' skills; they did not want the sinews of their valour to lose tautness and be infected by self-indulgence. Loathing a dainty style of living, they would harden body and mind with toil and endurance, spirits to act with a virile ruthlessness. They courted military celebrity so earnestly that you would have guessed they had unsexed themselves. Those especially who had forceful personalities or were tall and elegant embarked on this way of life. And if they were forgetful of their true selves they put toughness before allure, aimed at conflicts instead of kisses, tasted blood, not lips, sought the clash of arms rather than the arm's embrace, fitted to weapons hands which should have been weaving, desired not the couch but the kill, and those they could have appeased with looks they attacked with lances" (translated from *Saxo Grammaticus: History of the Danes*, trans. Peter Fisher and ed. Hilda Ellis Davidson [Cambridge: D. S. Brewer, 1979], 212). Hereafter cited as Fisher. On this passage, and on Saxo's shield maidens in general, see H. N. Holmqvist-Larsen, *Møer, skjoldmøer og krigere: En studie i og omkring 7. bog af Saxos Gesta Danorum* (Copenhagen: Museum Tusculanum, 1983), esp. ch. 4 ("Skjoldmødigressionen"). Holmqvist-Larsen makes a strong case for Saxo's familiarity with medieval traditions of *amazones* and *viragines* and his echoing of those traditions in the representation of his own shield maidens. There are, however, fundamental differences, from which we may conclude that Saxo's shield maidens are not derivative but stand on their own traditional feet. As Holmqvist-Larsen puts it, Saxo "omtolker det nordiske i lyset af det antikke" (45).

[2] See especially Vern L. Bullough, "Transvestites in the Middle Ages," *American Journal of Sociology* 79 (1974): 1381–94; John Anson, "The Female Transvestite in Early Monasticism: The Origin and Development of a Motif," *Viator* 5 (1974): 1–32; Max Gluckman, *Order and Rebellion in Tribal Africa* (New York: Free Press of Glencoe, 1963), introduction and ch. 3; and Victor Turner, *The Ritual Process: Structure and Anti-Structure* (Chicago: Aldine, 1969), ch. 3–5.

[3] Natalie Zemon Davis, *Society and Culture in Early Modern France* (Stanford: Stanford University Press, 1975), ch. 5.

[4] I understand the maiden-warrior theme to be a subtype of the shield-maiden theme. The latter term is used loosely in the literature to refer to any and all women who take up the sword or associate themselves with warfare or merely behave in unfeminine ways, however briefly and for whatever reason. Other subtypes of the shield maiden include the valkyrie, the avenging mother, and the maiden king (see n. 12 below). In Inger Boberg's *Motif-Index of Early Icelandic Literature*, Bibliotheca Arnamagnæana, 27 (Copenhagen: Munksgaard, 1966), examples are listed under

stories is that of Hervör, told in chapters 4 and 5 of *Hervarar saga ok Heiðreks*.[5] Hervör is the only child of Angantýr, who falls in battle before she is born. She is brought up in her maternal grandfather's household and quickly shows herself abler with bow, shield, and sword than with needlework. After a stint as a mugger (dressed and armed as a man, she kills people for their money), she learns who her father was and determines to seek out his grave on Samsey. "Bú þú at öllu," she says (in verse) to her mother, "sem þú son mundir" ("Equip me in all ways, as you would a son"); and under the name "Hervarðr" she joins up with, and eventually becomes head of, a band of Vikings. They come one day to Samsey, and at sunset Hervör makes her way on to the island, past a guardian, through the circle of flames, to her father's barrow. She enters and initiates the famous daughter-father verse dialogue known as the "Waking of Angantýr." The bone of contention is the sword Tyrfingr, which has gone to the grave with Angantýr. Hervör steadfastly insists, in the face of her father's wrath, prevarications, and prophecies of doom, that the sword is by rights hers, but Angantýr refuses to hand it over, claiming, among other things, that "no woman in the world would dare to hold it in her hand." In the end Hervör prevails, and armed with Tyrfingr re-enters the world of the living. She continues with her masculine adventures until, one day, she settles down, subsequently marries, and has two sons, of whom one, Heiðrekr, is the saga's main character.

The interpretation of this plot likely to spring first to the modern mind is a psychosexual one. Hervör is one of those women who wishes she weren't, and she repudiates her femaleness by taking on the appearance, behavior, and name of the male – she gives over, in the language of the tale, the needle for the sword. Symbolically seen, the struggle with her dead father over the sword is a struggle for phallic authority. Only when she comes to the point where she can have sons of her own (in psychoanalytic terms the proper resolution of the phallic conflict) does she resign herself to femaleness. So neat an example is Hervör's story of what Freud termed the masculinity complex that many readers will be tempted to let it stand there, as a crystalline realization of a human universal.

But is it so clear-cut? If we keep in mind that Hervör's story is not a case history but a fictional projection, and that it stands not alone but in a context of equivalent

---

F565.1 "Amazons. Woman warriors. Icelandic: 'skjaldmaer.' " For a recent, general discussion, focused on ballads, see Lise Praestgaard Andersen, *Skjoldmøer: En kvindemyte* (n.p.: Gyldendal, 1982); and Holmqvist-Larsen, *Møer, skjoldmøer og krigere*. Literary historians have yet to take into consideration the scanty but provocative archeological evidence for military women in the Germanic world. See especially Alfred Dieck, "Germanische Kriegerinnen: Literarische Erwäh-nungen und Moorleichenfunde," *Archäologisches Korrespondenzblatt* 5 (1975): 93–96; Hilda R. Ellis Davidson, *The Viking Road to Byzantium* (London: George Allen & Unwin, 1976), 114–15.

    [5] I have used the dual-language edition *Saga Heiðreks konungs ins vitra / The Saga of King Heidrek the Wise*, ed. and trans. Christopher Tolkien (London: Thomas Nelson & Sons, 1960). Tolkien bases his text on the *R* redaction, filling in the lacuna from *U* and supplying the end from *U/203*. References to other *fornaldarsögur* are to the edition of Guðni Jónsson, *Fornaldar sögur Norðurlanda*, 4 vols.(Reykjavík: Íslendingasagnaútgáfan, 1954; reprint, 1959), hereafter cited as *FSN*. Translations are my own unless otherwise indicated.

and linked plots, we may perceive her situation in a somewhat different light – a light more medieval than modern, and more anthropological than psychoanalytic. *Hervarar saga ok Heiðreks* is above all a narrative of genealogy and inheritance. It tells, in the main, the story of five generations: Arngrímr, who gets the sword Tyrfingr (depending on the version) either through marriage to Sigrlami's daughter or by slaying Sigrlami and seizing sword and daughter; his son Angantýr, who inherits it from Arngrímr; Hervör, who "inherits" it from her father Angantýr; her son Heiðrekr, who inherits from Hervör; and finally his son Angantýr, who avenges his father's death and retrieves the sword from his slayers.[6] Tyrfingr is thus more than a sword, more than a phallic symbol, and more than a literary binding device. It is the emblematic representation of the larger patrimony – not only treasures and lands, but family name and ancestral spirit – that each generation must secure for itself and pass on to the next. By generation, of course, is meant son or sons (or perhaps son- or sons-in-law), at least in the normal and preferable case. So it works in *Heiðreks saga* for four of the five generations. It is in the third generation that the line breaks:

Arngrímr	male
Angantýr	male
Hervör	female
Heiðrekr	male
Angantýr	male

The circumstances leading to this third-generation anomaly are clear enough. Hervör's father Angantýr was killed shortly after his marriage, and his pregnant wife gave birth to their one and only child. In the absence of brothers (and in the absence of paternal uncles, who were also slain, with Angantýr, on Samsey), Hervör thus stands as the sole survivor of her father's illustrious line. Hervör's own son Heiðrekr will also be illustrious, of course, as will *his* son Angantýr. For better or worse, then, the generation of Angantýr Arngrímsson and the generation of Heiðrekr must, if they are to be linked at all, be linked through Hervör, the sole representative of the intermediate generation. Herein lies the root explanation of Hervör's masculinity. So powerful is the principle of male inheritance that when it necessarily passes through the female, she must become, in legend if not in life, a functional son. The saga itself says as much. "Equip me as you would a *son*," she says to her mother as she readies herself to leave home in the quest for her father's grave. And the first thing she does when she confronts her dead father on Samsey is to state her relationship and her claim: "Vaki þú, Angantýr, / vekr þik Hervör, / eingadóttir / ykkr Sváfu; / seldu ór haugi / hvassan mæki, / þann er

---

6 This genealogy has been scrutinized by generations of scholars in an effort to pin down its historical background and relation to Continental and British sources. This line of inquiry does not concern us here (for a selective bibliography, see Tolkien's introduction, xxxvi–xxxviii) though we may note that more than one critic has concluded that Hervör Heiðreksdóttir is the original figure and that our Hervör (Angantýrsdóttir) is a fictional back formation. See especially Kemp Malone, "*Widsith* and the *Hervararsaga*," *PMLA* 40 (1925): 769–813, esp. 776–79.

Sigrlama / slógu dvergar" ("Wake, Angantýr; Hervor wakes you, the only daughter [=only child, female] of you and Svafa; give me, from the barrow, the keen blade, the one dwarves wrought for Sigrlami"). Chanting the names of her dead uncles and ancestors, she threatens to curse the entire line if she is not acknowledged as proper heir. To Angantýr's protestation that what she wants, the sword Tyrfingr, was taken by his slayers, she responds: "Segir þú eigi satt / . . . / trauðr ertu / arf at veita / eingabarni" ("You lie . . . you are loathe to grant the inheritance to your *only child*"), at which point the barrow opens and the flames blaze up. For his part, Angantýr repeatedly calls her *daughter*, even as he relinquishes the sword and grants her the strength (*afl*) and bold spirit (*eljun*) that are the legacy of Arngrímr's *sons*: "Far vel, dóttir, / fljótt gæfa ek þér / tólf manna fjǫr / ef þú trúa mættir, / afl ok eljun, allt it góða, / þat er synir Arngríms / at sik leifðu" ("Fare well, daughter; I would readily give you the life of twelve men – trust what I tell you – and the strength and bold spirit, all good things, that the sons of Arngrímr left after them").

Just what genetic notions underlie this and other genealogical stories in early Scandinavian literature is not clear, but I have the impression that the idea of latent or recessive features, physical or characterological, was undeveloped; inherited qualities seem to manifest themselves in some degree in every generation. The qualities that Angantýr now bestows as the "legacy of Arngrím's sons," *afl* and *eljun*, are emphatically "male" qualities. They may ultimately be "intended" for Hervör's future sons and their sons on down the line (as Angantýr himself points out) but in the meantime they must assert themselves in Hervör herself (as indeed they already have). As Hervör turns to leave the barrow, she utters a final stanza in which she blesses her father and refers to herself as "between worlds" ("helzt þóttumst nú / heima í millum, / er mik umhverfis / eldar brunnu" ["I seemed to myself to be between two worlds, as the fires burnt round me"]). Indeed she is between worlds: as the genetic conduit between the dead father and the unborn son, she bridges the worlds of male and female, living and dead, past and future. Only when she becomes fully nubile and hence ready to bear a male heir on whom the ancestral legacy will be unloaded, as it were, can Hervör withdraw from the male sphere and return to the female one. But until she is ready to produce another "son of Arngrímr," she must function, in the genealogical breach, as a "son of Arngrímr" herself.[7] It is a performance on which the heroic stature of her future son Heiðrekr, and of his sons and their sons, quite literally depends.[8]

Hervör may be the most elaborately drawn functional son in Norse literature, but she is by no means the only one. A similar story is played out on the mythological level by Skaði, who (as Snorri tells it) upon the death of her father

---

[7] I have confined myself here to those examples in which the genealogical breach is either explicit or unambiguously implied.

[8] Melissa Berman (Senior Thesis, Harvard University, 1977) makes the point that Hervör's narrative stint is very much like those of her male ancestors and progeny. "In every generation of the story, the problem of the hero's relationship to society is brought out through the repeating folk pattern of the fatherless hero's maturation, which seems always to involve an inability to deal with normal society, manifested by violence, unnatural acts, pride, and often, supernatural

Þjazi, "took helmet, byrnie, and a complete set of weapons and went to Ásgarðr to avenge her father" ("Skaði, dóttir Þjaza jǫtuns, tók hjálm ok brynju ok ǫll hervápn ok ferr til Ásgarðs at hefna fǫður síns").[9] She settles for a husband, Njǫrðr, but the marriage founders on the question of where to live. Njǫrðr wants to be near the sea, while Skaði "wanted to have the homestead her father had owned, in the mountains at the place called Þrymheimr" ("Skaði vill hafa bústað þann er átt hafði faðir hennar. Þat er á fjǫllum nǫkkurum, þar sem heitir Þrymheimr").[10] Snorri does not say in so many words that Skaði is a sole heir, but such is clearly implied by the fact that the task of vengeance and the paternal inheritance both devolve on her.

More explicit is the case of Þornbjörg in *Hrólfs saga Gautrekssonar*.[11] The only child of King Eirekr of Sweden and his wife ("Þau höfðu átt eina dóttur barna, sú er Þornbjörg hét" ["They had only one child, a daughter, who was called Þornbjórg"]), she spends her girlhood pursuing the martial arts. When her father objects to her masculine interests, she replies: "Nú með því at þú hefir eigi meir en eins manns líf til ríkisstjórnar ok ek er nú þitt einberni ok á allan arf eftir þik, má vera, at ek þurfi þetta ríki at verja fyrir konungum eða konungssonum, ef ek missi þín við" ("Now, because you have no more than one life to give to the governance of your kingdom, and also because I am your only child and sole heir, it may be that I will have to defend the land against other kings and princes, once you're gone" [ch. 4]). Her father provides her with men and lands; and she adopts male dress and name (Þórbergr) and is known as king. At this point in the story (as in several of the other cases), the warrior-maiden or functional-son theme merges with the maiden-king (*meykongr*) theme – the haughty woman who swears not to marry and defeats or kills her suitors.[12] The next several chapters are given over to the efforts, finally successful, of the hero Hrólfr Gautreksson to bend Þornbjörg to his will.

One of Saxo's several shield maidens is Ladgerda, whom Ragnar Shaggy-Breeks encounters on his visit to Norway shortly after the death of King Sivard.[13] Like other well-born Norwegian women, Ladgerda has assumed male dress for self-protection. Ragnar does not hesitate to make use of the military services of these female warriors in his quest for vengeance, and Ladgerda in particular

wisdom. These elements play a part in each of the four [main generational] units in *HSH*" (42). It might also be pointed out in this connection that in medieval medical thought, children were commonly believed, as Vern L. Bullough put it, "to resemble their fathers if the paternal seeds were stronger, the mother if the maternal ones were" ("Medieval Medical and Scientific Views of Women," *Marriage in the Middle Ages*, *Viator* 4 (1973): 497.

[9] *Edda Snorra Sturlusonar*, ed. Finnur Jónsson (Copenhagen: Gyldendal, 1931), 80–81 (here normalized).

[10] *Edda Snorra Sturlusonar*, 30.

[11] *FSN IV*, esp. ch. 4–5.

[12] Examples are collected and discussed in Erik Wahlgren, "The Maiden King in Iceland" (Ph.D. diss., University of Chicago, 1938). See also Boberg, *Motif-Index*, T311.4: "Maiden queen prefers to fight instead of marrying. She usually scorns or even kills her suitors or sets them difficult tasks."

[13] Saxo, bk. 9, 251–54; Fisher, 279–83.

proves "a skilled female fighter, who bore a man's temper in a girl's body; with locks flowing loose over her shoulders she would do battle in the forefront of the most valiant warriors" ("perita bellandi femina, quae virilem in virgine animum gerens, immisso humeris capillitio, prima inter promptissimos dimicabat"). Smitten with her (not least because she singlehandedly wins his war), Ragnar makes inquiries and learns that she is of high birth – indeed, is the daughter and sole survivor of the dead king. The rest of the story has to do with her resistance to his wooing (again the maiden-king motif) and their eventual marriage and divorce. Their son Fridleif becomes Earl of Norway and Orkney.

The Saxonian digression on amazons that heads this essay is prompted by the figure of Alfhild, who turns to male dress and the military life to avoid marrying an unwanted suitor. There is no question of a surrogate son here, for Alfhild's father is alive and she has two brothers. Her daughter Gyrid, however (for like other women of the maiden-king type, Alfhild does marry), finds herself at the end of a family line. "All these wars and critical events had so much depleted the Danish royal family," Saxo writes, "that eventually men realised it had been reduced to one woman, Gyrid, daughter of Alf and grandchild of Sigar" ("Talia rerum bellorumque discrimina adeo regiam apud Danos gentem exhauserunt, ut hanc ad solam Guritham, Alfi filiam, Sigari vero neptem, redactam esse constaret"). [14] The Danes appoint regents drawn from the populace, but when Gyrid saw that the "royal stock had dwindled to none but herself and there was no man of equal rank for her to marry, she declared a self-imposed oath of chastity, considering it preferable to forego a husband rather than select one from the rabble" ("Interea Alfi filia Guritha, cum regiam stirpem ad se solam redactam animadverteret neminemque, cui nuberet, nobilitate parem haberet, nuncupatis votis voluntariam sibi castimoniam indixit concubituque carere quam ex plebe maritum asciscere satius duxit").[15] Of Gyrid's military propensities Saxo says nothing until, years later, she dons male clothing and enters a battle next to her son. This after-the-fact behavior might on first glance seem to qualify Gyrid as loyal mother rather than surrogate son; but if we recall that Gyrid's mother too was a formidable warrior and that the martial nature in general tends to be passed down in the female line (witness Hervör's granddaughter Hervör and Brynhildr's daughter Áslaugr, both shield maidens in their own right),[16] we can safely assume that Gyrid was traditionally constituted as a maiden warrior from the outset, Saxo's order of events notwithstanding.

Finally there is Brynhildr herself, whose story is too well known to require summary here. Her case is, of course, greatly complicated by her literary popularity, which has left us with differing versions of her life and adventures. The picture that we get from the sources in general, and the *Völsunga saga* harmonization in particular, is a contradictory one. She is on the one hand

[14] Saxo, bk. 7, 200; Fisher, 219.

[15] Saxo, bk. 7, 202; Fisher, 222.

[16] See *Hervarar saga ok Heiðreks*, ch. 9 ("Hún [Hervör, daughter of Heiðrekr] var skjaldmær ok fæddist upp í Englandi með Fróðmari jarli") and *Þáttr af Ragnars sonum*, ch. 2.

depicted as an independent woman who lives in isolation, unencumbered by family of any kind; such a conception would indeed seem fundamental to her story. She is on the other hand depicted as a woman with a number of relatives, including a brother or brothers. According to Theodore M. Andersson, the former Brynhildr is the original one; her family, he argues, is *ersatz*, created in a late "speculative attempt to domesticate her in the style of other heroic stories":

> Germanic heroes and heroines regularly appear in the context of their families and are characteristically trapped in a situation that compels them to act against family obligations or interests. Hildebrand must kill his son. Angantýr must kill his brother. Rosimund and Signý must contrive the deaths of their husbands and Kriemhilt the death of her brothers. Gudrun must dispatch her sons Hamðir and Sǫrli to their deaths. Gunnarr must abandon his family to the bears and the wolves. Everywhere the immediate social context of the family focuses the tragedy. But Brynhild appears originally to have had no family. In *Þiðreks saga* she resides alone in a castle with her retainers. In the *Nibelungenlied* she is an independent princess on a remote island; the only signs of family are vague references to relatives in stanzas 476 and 526 and an adventitious uncle to whom she entrusts her realm in stanza 523. In Icelandic literature she does acquire a family: a father Buðli, a brother Atli, a sister Bekkhild, and a foster father Heimir. But here too she resides apart, in a tower or behind her magic flame wall, and the family looks like a late speculative attempt to domesticate her in the style of other heroic stories.[17]

If this is so, then we may posit that Brynhildr too was at some early layer in her development construed as a warrior maiden like Skaði or Hervör or Þornbjörg or Gyrid: the sole survivor who must function, in the genealogical breach, as a son.

"Sworn virgins" in Albania

The system of self- or clan government that existed in Iceland (and in early Germanic Europe in general) is a standard form of government in stateless societies.[18] Remarkably like the Icelandic case is that of Albania, where until quite recent times, feud was the chief or only mechanism for maintaining order.[19] Observers tell of retaliatory killings that go on for generations; of wergild successful and unsuccessful; of a hypersensitivity to matters of honor and slights

---

[17] Theodore M. Andersson, *The Legend of Brynhild*, Islandica 43 (Ithaca: Cornell University Press, 1980), 244.

[18] For a legal-anthropological study of Icelandic feud, see William Ian Miller, "Choosing the Avenger: Some Aspects of the Bloodfeud in Medieval Iceland and England," *Law and History Review* 1 (1983): 159–204.

[19] On feud in Albania, see especially M. Edith Durham, *High Albania* (London: Edward Arnold, 1901); the same author's *Some Tribal Origins, Laws, and Customs of the Balkans* (London: George Allen & Unwin, 1928); Margaret Hasluck, *The Unwritten Law in Albania*, ed. J. H. Hutton (Cambridge: Cambridge University Press, 1954); Ian Whitaker, "Tribal Structure

to personal and family prestige; of whetting/lamenting women and their flaunting of bloody tokens of the dead man before his living relatives; of male children raised from infancy with the imperative of revenge; of burnings-in; and of "sworn virgins" – women who for various reasons abandon the female role and assume the role of the male.

The existence, if not the exact social significance, of sworn virgins in Albania is well attested.[20] Dressed as men and often armed with rifles, and eating and smoking with men in public places, they have caught the curious eye of various travelers in various periods. Three related reasons are given for their renunciation of femaleness. One has to do with the rejection of an arranged marriage the young woman finds unacceptable; only by renouncing the female role altogether can she reject the marriage without bringing the respective families into feud. The second reason has to do with inheritance and is attested in the northern region of Malësia e Madje. Here a sonless man could prevail on his daughter (or, if he had two or more, the one of his choice) to assume the male role for inheritance purposes. He could then "bequeath to her his house and land for her lifetime, after which it reverted to the nearest male heir."[21] The third reason has to do with the obligations of bloodfeud. The role of women in Albanian feud was normally passive: they could be insulted, seduced, abducted, even murdered – but the business of revenge or seeking settlement always fell, at least in principle, to the male; women were, at least in theory though not always in practice, exempt from violence. In fact, numerous instances are recorded of women's seeking and taking revenge, often in quite gruesome forms. But such actions on the part of women were regarded not only as "illegal," but also, in some degree, as abnormal, embarrassing, and insulting.[22] There was, however, one set of circumstances in which a woman might play an active role in bloodfeud. As Ian Whitaker puts it, "When all of her brothers had been killed, she might herself assume the masculine role, abjure marriage, and take on the duty of exacting revenge for her siblings."[23] The sworn virgin then assumed male dress, and "having taken such an oath she might not revert to her earlier female role, but would thenceforth be treated solely as a man, killing and being killed in the bloodfeud and thereafter counting as a full life [as opposed to the usual half] in the calculation of blood money."[24] Just why women's lives were calculated at half a wergild is unclear; it may reflect either their relative value in that society or, as Whitaker suggests, an understanding that blood money might

---

and National Politics in Albania, 1910–1950" in *History and Social Anthropology*, ed. I. M. Lewis (London: Tavistock, 1968), 253–93; the same author's " 'A Sack for Carrying Things': The Traditional Role of Women in Northern Albanian Society," *Anthropological Quarterly* 54 (1981): 146–56.

[20] This discussion of sworn virgins is based mainly on Whitaker, " 'A Sack for Carrying Things' " (see also his bibliography), and Durham, *Some Tribal Origins*, 194–95.

[21] Durham, *Some Tribal Origins*, 195.

[22] See especially Hasluck, *The Unwritten Law of Albania*, 219–55.

[23] Whitaker, " 'A Sack for Carrying Things,' " 151.

[24] Whitaker, " 'A Sack for Carrying Things,' " 151.

be claimed by two clans.[25] In either case, a woman's assumption of a full wergild would seem to be an assumption of maleness on a fundamental level.

Let us pass over the first type of sworn virgin, the woman who rejects marriage (although we cannot help noting her resemblance to the maiden king), and turn instead to the woman who becomes a surrogate man for inheritance or feud purposes. What interests us here is that the assumption of the male role is prompted, in both cases, by a breach in the male line. Just how important the rule of father-son inheritance was in Albania is suggested by the once-widespread practice of levirate marriage there, whereby a man's widow was married by her late husband's brother and also whereby the resulting children might be credited to the dead brother, even though they be conceived after his death.[26] Better, evidently, to have a son who is not your own, or a son who is your daughter, than no son at all.

An interesting question for our purposes, but unfortunately one to which there appears to be no clear answer, is whether in reality these sworn virgins keep to their vows or whether (like their Icelandic literary sisters) they eventually marry and produce heirs of their own. In the case of the first category of male-women, the marriage-rejectors, the potential of feud would seem to constitute a powerful deterrent to eventual marriage (though even here at least one case of marriage has been recorded).[27] One might suppose that there would actually be an incentive for the women to marry in the other two cases, for they could then produce sons of their own and so restore the interrupted line of inheritance, but on this point the sources are, alas, scanty.[28] We must content ourselves with the observation that there exists a European society in which, traditionally, certain women under certain conditions renounce the female role, and dress, arm, and comport themselves as men; and further, that a certain proportion of them do so because they are brotherless and hence constrained to function as sons in the central matters of the patrilineage: feud and inheritance.

Icelandic law: *Baugatal*

The earliest Icelandic legal codex, *Grágás*, contains two schedules of compensation for slayings: *Baugatal* and *Vígslóði*. *Baugatal*, probably the older of the two, divides the kindred into four tiers depending on their relationship to the slain person. The first tier is composed of the near kinsmen of the slain person (father, son, brother, etc.) who are required to pay (if they are the defendants) or collect (if they are the plaintiffs) the main "ring" or lion's share of the wergild. Then comes the next tier made up of less immediately related kinsmen with a lesser

---

[25] Whitaker, " 'A Sack for Carrying Things,' " 150.

[26] Durham, *Some Tribal Origins*, 74; Whitaker, " 'A Sack for Carrying Things,' " 151.

[27] Durham, *Some Tribal Origins*, 195.

[28] Whitaker (" 'A Sack for Carrying Things,' " 151–52) argues that the oath of virginity was understood to be permanently binding (it was performed in the church), though he mentions cases in which it was broken.

share of the wergild, and so on. The extensive list, which explores all possible permutations of payers and receivers, consists exclusively of men, with one exception:

> Sú er ok kona ein er bæði skal baugi bœta ok baug taka *ef hon er einberni.* En sú kona heitir baugrygr. En hon er dóttir ins dauða, enda sé eigi skapþiggjandi til hǫfuðbaugs en bœtendr lifi, þá skal hon taka þrímerking *sem sonr,* ef hon tók eigi full sætti at vígsbótum *til þess er hon er gipt;* enda skulu frændr álengr taka. Nú er hon dóttir veganda, en engi er skapbœtendi til bœtendi til hfuðbaugs, en viðtakendr sé til, þá skal hon bœta þrímerkingi *sem sonr til þess er hon kømr í vers hvílu;* en þá kastar hon gjǫldum í kné frændum.[29]

> There is also one woman who is both to pay and to take a wergild ring, *given that she is an only child,* and that woman is called "ring lady." She who takes is the daughter of the dead man if no proper receiver of the main ring otherwise exists but atonement payers are alive, and she takes the three-mark ring *like a son,* given that she has not accepted full settlement in compensation for the killing, *and this until she is married,* but thereafter kinsmen take it. She who pays is the daughter of the killer if no proper payer of the main ring otherwise exists but receivers do, and then she is to pay the three-mark ring *like a son, and this until she enters a husband's bed* and thereby tosses the outlay into her kinsmen's lap.[30]

Not only is the daughter of a sonless, brotherless, and fatherless man expected to fill the genealogical breach, but also she is expressly said to do so *as a son* and even – since the clause specifically applies only to the unmarried – as a "maiden." That the practice is of some antiquity in Scandinavia is suggested by the presence of similar statutes in the early Norwegian laws.[31]

Nowhere in *Grágás* are the rules of bloodfeud spelled out. In Iceland, as elsewhere, these belong to the unwritten law. But insofar as a wergild list ranks an individual's kinsmen according to their degree of relatedness to the slain person, it may also be assumed to reflect, at least roughly, not only the schedule of inheritance but also the schedule of feud itself – the order, that is, in which the survivors are obliged to take retaliatory action. If this is so, then the very law – or at least one part of the law at one time – may be said to contemplate a situation

---

[29] *Grágás: Islœndernes lovbog i fristatens tid,* ed. Vilhjálmur Finsen (Copenhagen: Berling, 1852; reprint, Odense: Odense Universitetsforlag, 1974), 1:200–1 (normalization and italics mine).

[30] Translation from *Laws of Early Iceland: Grágás,* trans. Andrew Dennis, Peter Foote, Richard Perkins (Winnipeg: University of Manitoba Press, 1980), 181; my italics.

[31] *Gulaþing Law:* "Nú verðr kona baugrygr, verðr hon bæði arfa oðals ok aura ok á engi maðr undan henni at leysa . . . þær eru baugrygjar tvær dóttir ok systir, þaer skulu baugum bœta ok svá taka sem karlmenn, ok svá eigu þær boð á jǫrðum jafnt sem karlar. . . ." *Frostaþing Law.* "Nú er mær ein er baugrygr er kallaðr: hon skal bæði baugum bœta ok svá taka, ef hon er einberni ok til arfs komin, þar til er hon setzk á brúðstól, þá kastar hon gjǫldum aptr í kné frændum, ok skal hon hvárki siðan baugum bœta né taka. . . ." Text from *Norges gamle love indtil 1387,* ed. R. Keyser and P. A. Munch, 5 vols. (Oslo: C. Gröndahl, 1846), 1:92 and 1:184 respectively.

in which, in the absence of proper male heirs, a woman becomes a surrogate son not only in the transaction of wergild, but also in the matter of inheritance and also in the prosecution of feud.

Let me propose a hypothetical situation on the basis of *Baugatal* and other parts of Grágás, filling it out with familiars from the Icelandic sagas. A man is killed in bloodfeud and leaves a daughter, whom we will call Vígfús, as sole heir (as outlined in *Baugatal*). Let us say that Vígfús accepts wergild for her slain father but later, because of some further insult, ignores the settlement and seeks blood revenge.[32] She first tries to incite kinsmen to act on her behalf, but (as in *Eyrbyggja saga*) they refuse to accept responsibility. Disgusted, she arms herself and rides off with the intention of taking her own revenge; but she is foiled by a blizzard and returns home. She calms down, and there the matter rests. In the meantime, as a woman of means – for she is now the possessor of her father's patrimony and also his wergild – Vígfús has become an attractive marital candidate. In the absence of male relatives who would ordinarily arrange her marriage, she makes her opinion known to her remaining kinsmen – who, under the circumstances, are inclined to defer to her wishes. For her part, she is aware that to marry would mean that her father's wergild would become forfeit to her kinsmen and his patrimony subject to a husband's control. Her property, that which makes her sought after, also makes her choosy and even reluctant. She does finally marry, however – at which point her special status ceases and she becomes, in the eye of the law and the eye of the public, a woman like other women.[33]

In this scenario are found all the major themes of the maiden warrior (and maiden king) tales: brotherless daughter as heir; her pursuit of combat, especially in connection with revenge; her reluctance or refusal to marry (=maiden king); and her "disappearance" as a character once she does marry. Just when and where and how effectively *Baugatal*, with its "daughter clause," obtained in Iceland we do not know. Even when and where it did obtain, it cannot have affected very many women, and it may not have affected them in just the ways I have proposed here (it may be, for example, that I have underestimated the influence of the woman's remaining kinsmen over her property and her marriage). But if the Vígfús senario is even roughly valid as a collective description of women who did serve or might potentially serve as functional sons under the law, it provides an actual societal context for one conspicuous subtype of the shield-maiden complex.

---

[32] According to *Eyrbyggja saga* (ch. 38), women once had the right to serve as plaintiffs in court cases, but as the result of a botched performance ca. 992, they (and males under sixteen) were thenceforth debarred in that capacity.

[33] The idea that the virgin is more male than female – the idea, that is, that intercourse constructs the female – has a certain patristic authority. As Saint Jerome put it, "Quamdiu mulier partui servit et liberis, hanc habet ad virum differentiam, quam corpus ad animam. Sin autem Christo magis voluerit servire quam saeculo, mulier esse cessabit, et dicetur vir" ("As long as woman is for birth and children, she is different from man as body is from soul. But if she wishes to serve Christ more than the world, then she will cease to be a woman and will be called a man").

Conclusion

It is not without reason that the maiden warrior stories have been classified as fantasy. They are for the most part found in "fictional" sources; they bear, in their patterned representation of persons and events, the stigmata of folklore; and they are exaggerated to a greater or lesser degree. *Baugatal*, however, guarantees the "son" status of certain women under the law, and this piece of evidence, taken together with the analogous examples from Albania, leads us to the conclusion that while the tales may not be true as told, they are not purely fictional, either. They are best understood as imaginative adumbrations of a social reality in which certain women, under certain circumstances, became men for legal purposes. In other words: the maiden warrior tales spring from a feud society, like the Albanian one, in which a brotherless daughter was constrained to function, in the matters of the patrilineage, as a surrogate son.

Whether such daughters also became masculine in dress and behavior is another question. It seems on the one hand inevitable that the processes of legend would sooner or later conscript the woman who was, like Hervör, genealogically sandwiched between heroic forebears and heroic progeny: a female surrogate in the patrilineage would be *remembered* as acting out the role, whether she actually did or not. On the other hand, the lesson of the Albanian example is that the legal role can be acted out on the social level – or perhaps that the legal role implies the social role and is indistinguishable from it. Could this not also have been the case in Iceland? The woman contemplated in the *Baugatal* passage – the woman who transacts wergild and who, by extension, stands as heir and prosecutes bloodfeud – is, after all, a woman operating firmly within the male sphere. She may not be the amazon of legend, but neither is she Helga the Fair. She is a woman, as Hervör put it so neatly, between worlds. It is finally not so much her masculinity as her "betweenness" that had such a grip on the popular imagination.

It should be noted that the surrogate son, the woman I have argued is the historical prototype of the maiden warrior, does not herself choose the male role, but is, by custom and circumstance, chosen for it. This essay began with a discussion of the fantastic quality of the maiden warrior tales, so it is fitting to close it by suggesting that the real fantasy here is the dream of female autonomy. In the end these tales tell us less about daughters than they do about sons, and less about female volition than about the power, in Norse society, of the patrilineal principle to bend legend and life to its intention.

Pulzelle e maritate: Coming of Age, Rites of Passage, and the Question of Marriage in Some Early Italian Poems

Christopher Kleinhenz

At some point in the second half of the thirteenth century a young woman in Florence composed two complementary sonnets, in which she laments the custom in her society by which fathers are responsible for the betrothal and marriage arrangements of the female children in the family.[1] The author of these poems is known through the manuscript rubric as the Compiuta Donzella di Firenze, a descriptive title more than a name, but one that appears to reflect her education and fine poetic abilities.[2] The reactions of young women to these social practices concerning marriage arrangements probably ranged from humble acquiescence to varying degrees of happiness or sorrow, depending in large part on the qualities (physical, moral, spiritual), disposition, social status, and material condition of the *fidanzato / marito*. While the reasonably large corpus of medieval poetry

[1] For marriage practices in the Middle Ages, see, among others, the following studies: John F. Benton, "Clio and Venus: An Historical View of Medieval Love," in *The Meaning of Courtly Love*, ed. F. X. Newman (Albany: State University of New York Press, 1968), 19–42; Georges Duby, *Medieval Marriage: Two Models from Twelfth-Century France*, trans. Elborg Forster (Baltimore: Johns Hopkins University Press, 1978); Jack Goody, *The Development of the Family and Marriage in Europe* (Cambridge: Cambridge University Press, 1983); David Herlihy, *Medieval Households* (Cambridge, Mass.: Harvard University Press, 1985) and *The Social History of Italy and Western Europe, 700–1500: Collected Studies* (London: Variorum Reprints, 1978); Michael M. Sheehan, "Family and Marriage, Western European," in *Dictionary of the Middle Ages*, ed. Joseph R. Strayer (New York: Charles Scribner's Sons, 1984), 4: 608–12.

[2] These poems are contained only in the well known Vatican codex, Vat. Lat. 3793. We know virtually nothing about the author, except for what is disclosed in the sonnets themselves. She is the author of one other sonnet, written as part of a *tenzone* with an anonymous correspondent who first addresses her as "Gentil donzella somma ed insegnata" and later as "Compiuta Donzella." In two sonnets Maestro Torregiano praises a "donzella" for her "trovare dotta" ("being knowledgeable in writing poetry") and refers to this as a "marvelous event" ("maraviglia"). Guittone d'Arezzo addressed a letter (5) to a "Soprapiacente donna, di tutto compiuto savere, di pregio coronata, degna mia Donna Compiuta" (see *La Prosa del Duecento*, ed. Cesare Segre and Mario Marti [Milan-Naples: Ricciardi, 1959], 52). For an overview of the problems concerning the historical identity of the Compiuta Donzella and a review of the criticism, see Paolo Cherchi, "The Troubled Existence of Three Women Poets," in *The Voice of the Trobairitz: Perspectives on the Women Troubadours*, ed. William D. Paden (Philadelphia: University of Pennsylvania Press, 1989), 198–209.

classified as *chansons de malmariée* (It. *malmaritate*) records the complaint of unfortunate, ill-treated wives against their husbands, only a very few poems present what could be viewed, *mutatis mutandi*, as an earlier premarital manifestation of this same phenomenon: the unfortunate young woman who protests against patriarchal authority in matters of marriage.

The first sonnet by the Compiuta Donzella begins, as do many lyrics of the Duecento, with the *Natureingang*: it is spring, the time of rebirth, of joy and love, but the young woman experiences only sorrow. Her unhappiness does not stem from unreciprocated love, but is rather the result of her father's desire to find her a husband:[3]

> A la stagion che 'l mondo foglia e fiora
> acresce gioia a tut[t]i fin' amanti:
> vanno insieme a li giardini alora
> che gli auscelletti fanno dolzi canti;
> la franca gente tutta s'inamora,
> e di servir ciascun trag[g]es' inanti,
> ed ogni damigella in gioia dimora;
> e me, n'abondan mar[r]imenti e pianti.
> Ca lo mio padre m'ha messa 'n er[r]ore,
> e tenemi sovente in forte doglia:
> donar mi vole a mia forza segnore,
> ed io di ciò non ho disio né voglia,
> e 'n gran tormento vivo a tutte l'ore;
> però non mi ralegra fior né foglia.

> In the season when the world sends forth leaf and flower, joy increases in all noble lovers: they go together then to the gardens where the birds sing their sweet songs, the honest folk all fall in love, and each one strives to provide good service in matters of love, and every maiden dwells in a state of joy; but in me sadness and tears abound. For my father has given me cause for concern and keeps me always in a sad state: he wants to force a husband on me, and I have no desire or wish for this, and I continue to live in great torment; therefore, neither flower nor leaf gladdens me.

The sonnet is divided into two equal parts of seven verses each, the first half devoted to the joy of springtime and the second half to the sadness of the female protagonist. The palinodic symmetry of the composition is enhanced by the repetition of the initial dynamic verbal forms "foglia e fiora" in reverse, negative order in the final static substantive forms "fior né foglia."

In the second sonnet the Compiuta Donzella clarifies her desire and gives an

---

[3] The text of the poems follows Gianfranco Contini, ed., *Poeti del Duecento*, 2 vols. (Milan-Naples: Ricciardi, 1960), 1:434–35. The translation is mine.

unusual twist to the events. She does not wish a husband, but desires only to escape from the world and its falseness, to embrace the religious life of the convent, and to serve God:

> Lasciar vor[r]ia lo mondo e Dio servire
> e dipartirmi d'ogne vanitate,
> però che veg[g]io crescere e salire
> mat[t]ezza e villania e falsitate,
> ed ancor senno e cortesia morire
> e lo fin pregio e tutta la bontate:
> ond'io marito non vor[r]ia né sire,
> né stare al mondo, per mia volontate.
> Membrandomi c'ogn'om di mal s'adorna,
> di ciaschedun son forte disdegnosa,
> e verso Dio la mia persona torna.
> Lo padre mio mi fa stare pensosa,
> ca di servire a Cristo mi distorna:
> non saccio a cui mi vol dar per isposa.

> I would like to leave the world and serve God and depart from all vanity, because I see madness and uncourtliness and falseness increase and rise in prominence, while wisdom and courtliness and worthiness and goodness all decline and die: for which reason I would not want a husband or a lord, nor would I willingly remain in the world. When I recall that all men are intent on evil, I am very scornful of each one of them and turn myself toward God. My father makes me very upset and worried, for he turns me away from serving Christ: I do not know to whom he wants to give me as a bride.

The unresolved tension in these two poems is occasioned precisely because of the protagonist's questioning of and unwillingness to conform to certain social codes of behavior and institutions. As we know, medieval marriages were not unions necessarily based on any romantic sentiments; rather, nuptial arrangements generally reflected carefully calculated plans to join families in alliances and/or to consolidate property and other assets. Though unreliable as historical documents, the poems do disclose some of the problems and concerns that affected life in the Middle Ages.

The poems by the Compiuta Donzella are, I believe, unique in thirteenth-century Italian literature, and the plaintive voice that animates them takes its place alongside the many other lyric voices of the age. The most prevalent voice is that of the male *persona* who alternately laments and celebrates his amorous sentiments (the anguish and the joy), who praises his lady and her beauty and courtliness. Poems of departure and love from afar, poems of return and reunion, poems of uncertainty, jealousy, and tension – all of these themes and more are amply represented in the early Italian lyric. Women's voices, however, are a distinct minority, and the number of so-called "women's songs" are relatively few.[4] There are essentially five distinct female *personae* in thirteenth-century Italian lyric: (1) the *malmaritata* who complains about her unpleasant marital state (e.g., Compagnetto da Prato, "Per lo marito c'ho rio"); (2) the woman (married or not) who laments the departure of her husband/lover (e.g., Rinaldo d'Aquino, "Già mai non mi conforto"); (3) the dynamic equal partner in love/marriage who engages her lover/husband in a verbal duel (e.g., Giacomino Pugliese, "Donna, di voi mi lamento"); (4) the wise, generally older, often married and experienced woman who succeeds in maintaining the upper hand in the amorous relationship (e.g., Rustico Filippi, "Oi dolce mio marito Aldobrand-ino," and Cecco Angiolieri, " 'Becchin' amor!' 'Che vuo,' falso tradito?' "); and (5) the young woman who longs to have a husband and/or lover.[5]

In this essay I intend to consider those poems featuring the women in the last of these five categories, for they are in a special sense marginal. These women recognize their desire to have a lover or a husband; they are thus coming of age and view themselves as being at that particular moment in their life when they should either have a lover or get married in order to progress to a more advanced stage, to assume a new role in society, which, if their choice is marriage, would be that of the matron. They are, so to speak, on the margin, on one side of the line that separates them from assuming the role of wife and/or lover. They have come of age and are ready either to leave their inferior position in the family, subject to parental authority, or to move beyond their celibate existence, and to embark on what appears at least to be a freer and more fulfilling life as an adult. Several early Italian poems voice the sentiments of these women who eagerly anticipate the passage from their marginal position. Their eagerness may be explained in several ways: they wish (1) to assume a more responsible adult role in society; (2) to escape the often difficult conditions of their familial situation; (3) to engage in nuptially-sanctioned amorous activity without any social stigma; or (4) to follow and fulfill their desires as conditioned by nature and love without regard to the potentially dangerous social consequences of their acts.

The poems to be discussed in the following pages present in various ways the rites of passage signaled by this particular moment in human consciousness – the coming of age – and our investigation will be directed toward a greater appreciation of these sentiments and their various nuances in the poetry and toward making these interesting texts known to a wider audience.[6] We must remember, however, that these are literary artifacts – not historical documents – that have a place in the literary tradition and are conditioned therefore by stylistic and thematic

---

[4] For the general question of the woman's voice in medieval poetry with some references to Italian poetry, see Doris Earnshaw, *The Female Voice in Medieval Romance Lyric* (New York: Peter Lang, 1988).

[5] With regard to the fifth category, the Compiuta Donzella di Firenze longs for precisely the opposite, or perhaps better for the spiritual version of the human relationship: to become a bride of Christ by entering a religious order.

[6] It is fair to say that these poems are relatively unknown even within the general field of Italian studies and that they have not been analyzed or discussed as a group in the manner that I propose.

conventions. Moreover, these poems do not necessarily reflect a specific historical event, nor were they, generally speaking, written by women.[7]

In the *canzonetta* "Ormai quando flore" Rinaldo d'Aquino presents the
monologue of a young female protagonist who experiences the first stirrings of
love and sexual passion.[8] It is spring, as the *Natureingang* indicates, and all the
elements of nature combine to create an atmosphere conducive to love:[9]

> Ormai quando flore
> e mostrano verdura
> le prate e la rivera,
> li auselli fan sbaldore
> dentro da la frondura
> cantando in lor manera:
> infra la primavera, – che ven presente
> frescamente – così frondita,
> ciascuno invita – d'aver gioia intera.   (1–9)

> Now when flowers appear and the fields and countryside show
> forth their green, the birds make joyous sounds in the branches
> singing in their fashion: in springtime which will soon be here
> with its fresh foliage, everyone is bidden to have complete joy.

Seeing the rebirth of nature, hearing the symphony of birds and smelling the sweet
scent of flowers, the woman joins in this universal movement toward amorous
fulfillment and notes the one crucial difference between herself and the natural
world: unlike wood, her heart will burn with the fires of passion and never be
consumed:[10]

> Quando l'aloda intendo
> e rusignuol vernare
> d'amor lo cor m'afina,
> e magiormente intendo
> ch'è legno d'altr'affare
> chè d'arder no rifina.
> Vedendo quell'ombrina – del fresco bosco,

---

[7] The number of women writers in Italy in the thirteenth and fourteenth centuries is very
small, unlike the relatively rich tradition of the Provençal *trobairitz*.

[8] Very little is known about Rinaldo d'Aquino, except that he was attached to the court of
Emperor Frederick II in Sicily in the first half of the thirteenth century and that he appears to be
a member of the same family as St. Thomas Aquinas, perhaps even his brother. Another of his
poems – "Già mai non mi conforto" – has as its protagonist a woman who laments the departure
of her lover on the Crusades.

[9] The text with slight modifications follows Bruno Panvini, ed., *Le rime della scuola siciliana*
(Florence: Leo S. Olschki, 1962), 115–16. The translation is mine.

[10] The scene is charged with sexual metaphors: in the analogy between the landscape and the
human body, the "ombrina del fresco bosco" would be the woman's pubic area, and her realization
of developmental changes there lead her to the conclusion that she will soon experience the climax
of that growth process in coitus.

> ben cognosco – ca cortamente
> serà gaudente – l'amore che mi china. (19–27)

> When I hear the lark and the nightingale sing at the beginning
> of spring, my heart is refined by love, and I understand to a
> greater degree that it is made of a different sort of wood that
> never stops burning. Seeing the little shadow cast by the new
> foliage in the woods, I well know that the love that overcomes
> me will soon have its joy.

Acknowledging that she is loved by another, she admits that she has never been
in love before, but the advent of spring has changed all that. She finds herself,
then, at that special turning point in her life, and this coming of age presents a
dilemma: does she yield to the enticements of her doting *fante* and to her own
emotions? or does she hold firm against the onslaught of desire?

> [Mi] china, ch'eo so amata,
> e già mai non amai:
> ma 'l tempo mi 'namura
> e fami star pensata
> d'aver mercè ormai
> d'un fante che m'adura;
> e saccio che tortura – per me sostene
> e gran pene. – L'un cor mi dice
> che si disdice, – e l'altro mi sicura. (28–36)

> Love overcomes me, for I am loved and never before have I
> loved: but the season causes me to fall in love and to believe
> that I will soon have the affection of a young man who adores
> me; and I know that he suffers great pain and torment because
> of me. On the one hand, my heart says it is not the proper thing
> to do, but, on the other hand, it gives me reassurance.

The solution to her dilemma does not lie in marriage – indeed, marriage is never
mentioned in the text – but rather in following her own instincts and natural
inclinations. Appearing to be in complete control of the situation, she makes a
bold request to her suitor that he not do anything to harm her reputation and that
he agree to the conditions she sets forth for their relationship, which must be both
open and honest:

> Però prego l'amore,
> che mi 'ntende e mi svoglia
> come la foglia vento,
> che no mi faccia fore
> quel che presio mi toglia
> e stia di me contento.
> Quelli c'à intendimento – d'avere intera
> gioia e c[i]era – de l[o] mio amore
> senza romore, – no nde à compimento. (37–45)

Therefore, I ask my love, who loves me and moves me like the
wind does a leaf, that he not do anything to me in public that
would take away my honor and that he be satisfied with what I
want. Whoever wants to have both the external sign of my love
and complete joy in private will not be satisfied.

The emphasis on the necessary public nature of the relationship perhaps reflects
not only the sense of personal moral probity on the part of the woman, but also
a conscious desire to avoid gossip harmful to one's reputation as well as the
potential problems in informal, secret marriages. The message to the *fante* is clear:
he must make the proper sort of commitment to her or else there will be no
consummation of their love.

Although not mentioned directly in Rinaldo's text, marriage is a fundamental
element in other poems. The anonymous *canzonetta* "Part'io mi cavalcava"
provides a narrative frame for the dialogue between a mother and her sexually
active daughter. The young woman takes her mother to task for not having yet
given her a husband:[11]

> . . . "Oi madre bella,
> lungo tempo è passato
> ch'io degio aver marito,
> e tu non lo m'ài dato;
> quest'è malvagio invito,
> ch'io soffro, tapinella." (4–9)

"O lovely mother dear, much time has passed and I must have
a husband, and you have not given him to me; this is a bad
prohibition that I am suffering, o wretched me."

The mother (20–27) observes that the daughter is still in the prime of youth and
that sufficient time remains for her to marry. However, the younger woman, to
emphasize her point, describes the intensity of her passionate desire with a
remarkable image:

> . . . "io tutta ardo e 'ncendo.
> La voglia mi domanda
> cosa che nom[ar] suole
> una luce [miranda],
> ch'è più chiara che 'l sole;
> per ella vo languendo." (31–36)

"I am all afire. My desire demands what is usually called a
wonderfully brilliant light that is brighter than the sun; because
of this light and its power I am languishing."

The description of the intense and marvelously beautiful light accompanying and

---

11 The text follows Panvini, 534–37. The translation is mine.

perhaps resulting from her desire suggests the physiological phenomenon of an orgasm. Her mother immediately recognizes the explicit sexual nature of this image and understands that her daughter has first–hand knowledge of sexual pleasure. She expresses her double sense of dismay and scandal in the following stanza:

> "Oi figlia, non pensai
> sì fosse mala tosa,
> chè ben conosco ormai
> di che se' golïosa;
> chè tanto n'ài parlato
> non s'avene a pulcella,
> credo che l'ài provato,
> sì ne sai la novella.
> Lascioti, dolorosa." (37–45)

> "O daughter, I did not think that you were such a bad girl, for I fully understand now what makes you so eager; for you have spoken about it much more than is suitable for a maiden, and thus I believe that you have experienced it, so well you know its unique properties. I leave you, sorrowful one."

In her vituperative response the daughter bitterly denounces her parent and, at the same time, offers a rapturous hymn of praise to the wondrous pleasures of carnal passion:

> "Oi vecchia trenta cuoia,
> non mi stare in tenzone,
> se [non] vuoli ch'io muoia
> o perda la persone;
> chè lo cor mi sollaza
> membrando quella cosa
> che le donne sollaza,
> per ch'amor ne riposa,
> ed io ne sto 'n arsione!" (46–54)

> "O wretched old and wrinkled woman, don't argue with me, if you do not want me to die or lose my beauty; for my heart is gladdened when I think about that thing that makes women happy, by means of which love is put to rest, but I continue to burn with desire!"

The highly charged sexuality that pervades these verses, together with the dynamic give and take of the dialogue, accurately reflects the hormonal changes that signal the coming of age and the inter-generational conflict that generally accompanies it. The familial situation presented here is indeed universal in its interpretation and application. Plus ça change . . . .

Two poems on this same theme, both *ballate* and in dialogue form, are found among the so-called "rime dei Memoriali Bolognesi," that remarkable collection of notarial documents and vernacular verse in the Bolognese civic archive.[12] One poem relates the complaint of a daughter directed toward her father, who has not yet found her a husband:[13]

"Babbo meo dolce, con' tu mal fai,
ched io sum grande, marito no me dài.
Mal fa' tu, babo, che no me mariti
ched io son grande e son mostrata a dite.
Ben m'ài tenuta cum tego asai:
fa 'l per De' ora, s' tu 'l di' far çamai."

"Figlola mia, non ti far meravegl[i]a
s'io t'ò tenuta cotanto in famegl[i]a,
c'on dal to fatto ancor non trovai,
ch' al sper de Deo trovaròlo ogimai."

"El m'è sì forte cresciuta la vogl[i]a
d'andar atorno ch'eo me 'n moro di dogl[i]a.
Babbo meo dolce, fa' con' tu sai
che 'l meo cor tristo ralegri ogimai."

"Sweet Daddy mine, how bad you are, for I am grown up and you aren't giving me a husband."

"You are doing a bad thing, daddy, in not marrying me, for I am grown up and they are pointing at me. You have kept me with you for a long time; do it now by God, if you are ever going to do it."

"Daughter of mine, don't be amazed that I have kept you for such a long time in the family, for a man worthy of you I have not yet found but by hoping in God, I will find him soon."

"So great has my desire grown to leave the house that I am dying of sorrow. Sweet Daddy mine, do what you can so that my sad heart will be gladdened soon."

The young girl is aware of her physical development – she knows that she has become the object of attention – and the father also recognizes his obligation to her. His protective attitude toward her is disclosed by the high standards he has for her future husband: no one yet has matched her fine qualities. Nevertheless, the intensity of her emotions makes it imperative for the father to act rapidly.

---

[12] For the history of the formation of the Memoriali Bolognesi and the lyrics contained therein, see the following studies: Adriana Caboni, *Antiche rime italiane tratte dai Memoriali Bolognesi* (Modena: Società Tipografica Modenese, 1941); Giosue Carducci, "Intorno ad alcune rime dei secoli XIII e XIV ritrovate nei Memoriali dell'Archivio Notarile di Bologna," in *Studi sulla letteratura italiana dei primi secoli*, vol. 8 of the Edizione Nazionale delle Opere di Giosue Carducci (Bologna: Zanichelli, 1945), 169–343; Santorre Debenedetti, "Osservazioni sulle poesie dei Memoriali Bolognesi," *Giornale storico della letteratura italiana*, 125, fasc. 371 (1948): 1–41; and H. Wayne Storey, "The Editorial Redefinition of Margins: The *Memoriali bolognesi* and the Literary Culture of Chigiano L. VIII. 305," ch. 3 in his *Transcription and Visual Poetics in the Early Italian Lyric* (New York: Garland, 1993), 111–70.

[13] The text of the poem follows Contini, 1: 784. The translation is mine.

The other *ballata* on this subject in the Bolognese collection, "Mamma, lo temp' è venuto," presents a dialogue between a mother and her daughter, who has her heart set on getting married. The mother voices her concerns, among which the possibility of premature death – "tosto podriss' esser morta" (31) – would appear to refer to the daughter's young age and lack of physical maturity ("la persona non ài," "you do not have the body," 30) for the inevitable dangers in childbearing. However, these rational objections do not sway the young woman who is completely consumed with sexual desire, as the final stanza indicates:[14]

> "Matre, tant ò 'l cor açunto,
> la vogl[i]a amorosa e conquisa,
> ch'aver voria lo meo drudo
> vixin plu che non è la camixa.
> Cun lui me staria tutta nuda
> né mai non voria far devisa:
> eo l'abraçaria en tal guisa
> che 'l cor me faria allegrare." (37–44)

> "Mother, so greatly is my heart struck by conquering amorous desire that I would want to have my lover even closer to me than my blouse/slip. With him I would be completely naked, and never would I want to separate myself from him: I would embrace him in such a way that would make my heart happy."

The very sensuous, erotic references in this stanza are not uncommon in the relatively large body of "realistic" or "popular" poetry of the period and stand as reminders of the multifaceted nature of this "non-courtly" literary production. To be sure, even in its seeming "spontaneity" and "immediateness" – characteristics that attracted the admiration of more romantically inclined critics in both the previous and the current century – this so-called "poetry of the people" adhered to certain stylistic and thematic conventions and norms.

The poems presented above are all concerned with the female protagonist's awareness of her coming of age and her concomitant desire to have a husband/lover. Two other poems from the early Itàlian lyric tradition demonstrate a certain affinity to this theme, while not adhering to the basic pattern. In the *canzone* "L'amor fa una donna amare" by Compagnetto da Prato, the female *persona* is so consumed by passion that she willingly and knowingly goes against social conventions by taking direct and decisive action in soliciting the attention of her lover.[15] The poem discloses nothing of her personal circumstances, only that she is reduced to a desperate state by love; in this regard it is similar to Rinaldo

---

[14] The text of the poem follows Contini, 1: 770–72. The translation is mine.

[15] We know virtually nothing about this poet who appears to have been attached in some capacity to the Imperial Court of Frederick II in Sicily. For a fine study of Compagnetto's poetry, see Anna Granville Hatcher, "Compagnetto da Prato: A Sophisticated Jongleur," *Cultura neolatina*, 19, nos. 1–2 (1959), 35–45.

d'Aquino's "Ormai quando flore." In the progression of stanzas we can see the evolution of her thought processes as she deliberates the propriety of her actions:[16]

> L'amor fa una donna amare.
> Dice: "Lassa, com faragio?
> Quelli a cui mi voglio dare
> non so se m'à 'n suo coragio.
> Sire Dio, che lo savesse
> ch'io per lui sono al morire,
> o c'a donna s'avenesse:
> manderia a lui a dire
> che lo suo amor mi desse.
>
> "... Dio! l'avessero in usanza
> l'altre di 'nchieder d'amare!
> ch'io inchiedesse lui d'amanza,
> chè m'à tolto lo posare;
> per lui moro for fallanza." (1–9, 14–18)

> Love makes a woman love. She says: "Alas, what will I do? I do not know if the one to whom I want to give myself has me in his heart. Lord God, if only he knew how I am dying on account of him, or if only it were appropriate for a lady to do: I would send him a message asking for his love.
> "... God! if only other women were in the habit of asking for love! if only I could ask him for love, for he has taken away my rest; I will die without fail on his account."

The abrupt authorial opening provides the frame for the monologue which becomes, in the end, a dialogue. While part of the general tradition of the *chanson de femme*, this poem reflects, I believe, a specific interest in the rites of passage under examination here, indeed, in the reshaping and redefining of these rites as they apply to the female *persona* and to her alone. The woman is very conscious of the non-traditional nature of her thoughts and actions, and finds herself in a marginal position, ready to embark upon uncharted waters, to do what women do not usually do, to act in new and unconventional ways. In the next stanza she presents the steps that lead to her resolution to take the initiative and send for her lover:

> "Donne, no 'l tenete a male,
> s'io danneo il vostro onore,
> chè 'l pensier m'à messa a tale
> convenmi inchieder d'amore.
> Manderò per l'amor mio,
> saprò se d'amor mi 'nvita;
> se non, gliela dirabo io

---

16 The text follows Panvini, 231–32. The translation is mine.

> la mia angosciosa vita.
> Lo mio aunore non disio."(19–27)

> "Ladies, do not take it badly if I harm your honor, for the
> thought has brought me to such a point that I must ask for love.
> I will send for my love, I will learn if he welcomes me with love;
> if not, I will tell him about my sorrowful life. I do not desire my
> honor."

She is willing to give up everything – self-respect, reputation, honor – for love. The result – thanks to the god of Love's intervention – is immediate and satisfying, for the lover miraculously appears on the scene and together they consummate their love:

> "Dimmi s'è ver l'abrazzare
> che mi fai, donna avenente,
> chè sì gran cosa mi pare,
> creder no 'l posso neiente."
> "Drudo mio, se Dio mi vaglia
> ch'io del tuo amor mi disfaccio,
> merzè, non mi dar travaglia!
> Poi che m'ài ignuda in braccio,
> meo sir, tenemi in tua baglia!"   (46–54)

> "Tell me if it's true this embrace that you are giving me,
> lovely lady, for it seems to be such a great thing that I cannot
> believe it at all."
> "Lover boy, with God as my witness I am dying for your
> love, please, don't give me any problems! Since you have me
> naked in your arms, my lord, hold me in your power!"

There is no talk of, no wish for marriage; the only lament the woman voices is that of unrequited desire, which is soon satisfied. Unlike the other poems discussed above, the tension which marks the beginning of this poem quickly dissolves by the final stanzas, as a consequence of the sort of instant gratification provided by the sudden, welcome appearance of the male figure. The rapid resolution to the woman's dilemma in Compagnetto da Prato's poem stands in sharp contrast to the intricate argumentation found in Cielo d'Alcamo's *contrasto* "Rosa fresca aulentissima," although the end in both poems in the same: the consummation of sexual desire. The remainder of this essay will be devoted to Cielo's poem.[17]

The Italian phrase in the title of this essay – *pulzelle e maritate* ("maidens and wives") – comes from this early debate poem, which presents a dialogue between a man and a woman. As a consequence of its form, Cielo's *contrasto* lacks

---

[17] We know very little about Cielo d'Alcamo's life. His poem "Rosa fresca aulentissima" is cited by Dante Alighieri in *De vulgari eloquentia* (1.12.6) as an example of the more popular Sicilian dialect, which would be unworthy of consideration as the illustrious literary language of Italy.

therefore some of the plaintive or reflective qualities of a monologue; moreover, unlike some of the poems discussed above, this one does not disclose the woman's thought processes as she confronts the problems posed by her coming of age. Nevertheless, like the other female *personae* we have observed, this one definitely wants to get married and to enjoy the sexual pleasures that come with this new social state. The poem provides brilliant examples of subtle word play, finely hewn images, and dynamic characterization and represents a distinctly Italian version of the *pastourelle* genre. Although its intrinsic merits would warrant an attentive and exhaustive analysis, I will, given the limitations of space, consider primarily those passages concerned with the subject of marriage.

The protagonists of the *contrasto* are an itinerant *jongleur* and a woman of the Sicilian bourgeoisie. They engage in an amorous debate, a sort of verbal duel with the two combatants striving toward the same goal but from different perspectives. Both desire sexual intimacy, with the difference being that the man wants it without benefit of clergy, while the woman will welcome it only within the sanctified state of matrimony – or at least so she claims. This is then the bone of contention, the basis for the verbal conflict and the motive force for the entire poem. Proposals and counter-proposals, arguments and counter-arguments mark the movement of this conversation, rich in erotic innuendoes and sexually oriented *double-entendres*, which gradually build to a dramatic conclusion.[18]

In the initial verses the male *persona* refers to the extreme desirability and beauty of the woman: "Rosa fresca aulentissima, – c'apari inver la state, / le donne ti disïano – pulzell' e maritate" ("Fresh, most fragrant rose, that appears in the summer, women – maidens and wives – desire you").[19] In the next three verses he describes his desperate state because of love: "tra[ji]mi de ste focora – se t'este a bolontate; / per te non aio abento notte e dia, / penzando pur di voi, madonna mia" ("remove me from these fires if it pleases you; for you I have no rest night and day, thinking only of you, my lady," 3–5). Despite the lofty aristocratic and rhetorically correct phrasing, the woman understands the not terribly well concealed carnal nature of the man's desire and immediately goes on the offensive; nevertheless, in her refusal she introduces several elements that are central to the poem's imagistic and conceptual structure: (1) the notion of the madness of love (*follia*) and its adverse effects; (2) the double metaphor of plowing the sea and sowing seeds, while obviously belonging to the class of

---

[18] The poem is composed of 160 verses arranged in five-line stanzas of three mono-rhymed *doppi settenari* (double heptameters) and two mono-rhymed hendecasyllables. The *contrasto* has not been the subject of much critical commentary. See, among others, Gianfranco Folena, "Cultura e poesia dei Siciliani," in *Le origini e il Duecento*, vol. 1 of *Storia della letteratura italiana*, ed. Emilio Cecchi and Natalino Sapegno (Milano: Garzanti, 1965), 328–37; Angelo Monteverdi, "*Rosa fresca aulentissima . . . tragemi d'este focora*," in *Studi e saggi sulla letteratura italiana dei primi secoli* (Milan-Naples: Ricciardi, 1954), 103–23; Antonino Pagliaro, "Il Contrasto di Cielo d'Alcamo," in his *Poesia giullaresca e poesia popolare* (Bari: Laterza, 1958), 193–232; and F. A. Ugolini, "Problemi della *Scuola poetica siciliana*: nuove ricerche sul *Contrasto* di Cielo d'Alcamo," *Giornale storico della letteratura italiana*, 115 (1940): 161–87.

[19] The text follows Panvini, 169–76. The translation is mine.

impossibilia, has very evident sexual overtones; (3) the presentation of wealth and earthly riches as a determining factor in human relationships and the basis for marital contracts; and (4) the alternative to secular life – the withdrawal to a nunnery:[20]

> Se di mevi trabagliti, – follia lo ti fa fare,
> lo mar potresti arompere, – avanti, a semenare,
> l'abere de sto secolo – tutto quanto asembrare,
>   avereme non poteri a esto monno;
>   avanti li cavelli m'aritonno.   (6–10)

If you are troubled by me, madness makes you so; you could plow the sea and sow seeds, you could gather all earthly riches, but you could never have me in this world; I would cut my hair first.

Stanzas two and three, as many others in the *contrasto*, are linked by the metrical device known as *coblas capfinidas*, which is a particularly effective way of facilitating the movement of thoughts, images, and ideas throughout much of the poem. The man begins by reiterating the woman's pledge to cut her hair, but the phrase forms the first part of a conditional sentence. In this way he succeeds in shifting the focus from the spiritual significance of the tonsure to the sensual loss it would represent. Moreover, by stressing carnal pleasure, the man reduces the woman from the sweet-smelling, aesthetically pleasing rose of the first line ("rosa fresca aulentissima") – one to be admired and desired, but not touched – to a commercial, garden variety rose to be plucked and enjoyed – "rosa fresca de l'orto" (13). He states his objective blatantly but hypothetically by proposing that they make love:

> Se li cavelli artonniti, – avanti foss'io morto,
> [donna], c'aisì mi perdera – lo sollacc[i]o e 'l diporto.
> Quando ci passo e veioti, – rosa fresca de l'orto,
>   bono conforto donimi tuttore:
>   poniamo che s'aiunga il nostro amore.   (11–15)

If you cut your hair, I would rather die, my lady, for in this way I would lose joy and pleasure. When I pass by and see you, fresh rose of the garden, you always give me good comfort: let's suppose that we consummate our love.

The woman repeats these final suggestive words but only to negate the possibility they present and then refers to her family and the threat they represent

---

[20] In this regard it is appropriate to recall that the sonnets by the Compiuta Donzella di Firenze, with which this essay began, proposed withdrawal from the world as the only "solution" to the problem of overbearing parental authority in the selection of a husband. Here, of course, the issue is completely different: the woman wants a husband and will not yield to the man's sexual entreaties without being married first.

to her would-be suitor. Anyone familiar with Sicilian family structures, allegiances, and vendettas will understand the gravity of her words:

> Che 'l nostro amore aiungasi – no boglio m'atalenti.
> Se ci ti trova paremo – co gli altri miei parenti!. . .
> Guarda no s'ar[i]colgano – questi forti correnti!
> > Como ti seppe bona la venuta,
> > consiglio che ti guardi a la partuta. (16–20)

I do not want to be attracted by the thought that we might consummate our love. If my father and my other relatives find you here. . . . Be careful that these fast runners not seize you. Since you found the coming here easy, I caution you on your leaving.

However, this warning is easily turned to the man's advantage, thanks to his knowledge of the legal system established by Emperor Frederick II. The Constitutions of Melfi, promulgated in 1231, have provisions regarding punishments and fines for varieties of assault and for the illegal bearing and use of arms:[21]

> Se i tuoi parenti trovanmi, – e che mi pozon fari?
> Una difensa mettoci – di dumili' agostari:
> non mi toccàra pàdreto – per quanto avere ambari.
> > Viva lo 'mperadore graz[i'] a Deo!
> > Intendi, bella, che ti dico eo? (21–25)

If your family members find me, what can they do to me? I'll slap a fine on them of 2,000 *agostari*. Your father would not be able to touch me no matter how much wealth he might amass. Long live the Emperor, thanks be to God! Do you understand, beautiful one, what I'm telling you?

The woman's response demonstrates that she has not grasped the significance of his words. Rather, she focuses on his reference to wealth and uses this opportunity to clarify and enhance her own financial position. However, in so doing, she discloses her own foolishness, for the two persons cited in her comparison – the Soldano and the Saladino – are, in fact, one and the same! Her overriding concern with wealth has caused her to misinterpret the man's words as his statement of

---

[21] See Book 1, Titles 10–19 of *The Liber Augustalis or Constitutions of Melfi Promulgated by the Emperor Frederick II for the Kingdom of Sicily in 1231*, trans. James M. Powell (Syracuse: Syracuse University Press, 1971). In Title 16 of Book 1 we read of the importance of invoking the Emperor's name: "The authority of the law of nations has introduced that each man should be permitted to protect his own body, and natural reason does not find this abhorrent. Yet, because it often happens that the power of an attacker is so great that even if the victim is allowed to defend himself he cannot actually do so, by the authority of the present law we grant every man permission to defend himself against his attacker by the invocation of our name. He should forbid him by the imperial office to dare to attack him further" (18–19). The reference to the two thousand *agostari* as a penalty appears to be hyperbolic.

personal wealth and to object that he cannot, as it were, buy her and her affection.
She is not a prostitute, nor is she a destitute fortune hunter:

> Tu me no lasci vivere – nè sera, nè maitino.
> Donna mi son di perperi – d'auro massamotino.
> Se tanto aver donassemi – quanto à lo Saladino
>   e per aiunta quant'à lo Soldano,
>   toccareme non poteri a la mano.   (26–30)

> You do not let me live in peace night or day. I am a very wealthy
> lady. If you were to give me all that belongs to the Saladino and,
> in addition, all that the Soldano has, you could not even touch
> my hand.

The woman's failure to understand the meaning of his reference to money
occasions the man's misogynistic diatribe against the foolishness and suscepti-
bility of women. At the end of the stanza the man encourages her to concede
victory to him, to yield to him, for that pattern of subjugation follows the natural
order of things. And if she does not act according to nature, then she might regret
("repent") her actions:

> Molte sono le femmine – c'ànno dura la testa,
> e l'omo con parabole – l'adimina e amonesta,
> tanto intorno procazzale – fin che l'à in sua podesta.
>   Femmina d'omo non si può tenere:
>   guardati, bella, pur de ripentere.   (31–35)

> Many women have a hard head, and a man can dominate and
> counsel them with words, and pursue them until they are in his
> power. A woman cannot keep herself away from a man: be
> careful, beautiful one, only to avoid regrets ("repentance").

Regret (repentance) for not following her natural sexual inclination is the
farthest thing from the woman's mind; indeed, she is concerned primarily that
other good women may not receive reproach because of any actions on her part.[22]
By identifying the man by his occupation – *canzoneri*, a jongleur – , she appears
to be suggesting that class distinctions separate them, she, of course, being of
higher social station:

> Ch'eo ne [ri]pentesseme? – Davanti foss'io aucisa!
> ca nulla bona femmina – per me fosse riprisa.
> [A]ersera passastici – correnno a la distisa.
>   Aquetiti, riposa, canzoneri,
>   tue parabole a me non piaccion gueri.   (36–40)

---

[22] This concern is also present in the *canzone* by Compagnetto da Prato, "L'amor fa una donna
amare," in which the woman, recognizing that social conventions require that women not be
aggressive in their amorous demands, goes against these strictures, so enamored is she! See the
discussion of the poem above.

Why ever should I have regrets (repent)? I'd rather be killed than have any good woman be blamed because of me. Yesterday evening you went by at a fast pace. Calm down, rest a bit, jongleur, I do not like your words at all.

The man then turns on the charm and uses words and phrases that are intended to convince the woman of the sincerity of his affection; indeed, their love would seem to be inevitable, a product of destiny:

> Quante sono le schiantora – che m'à[i] mise a lo core!
> E solo purpenzannome – la dia quanno vo fore,
> femmina de sto secolo – tanto no amai ancore
> quant'amo teve, rosa invidïata.
> Ben credo che mi fosti distinata.   (41–46)

So many pains you've put in my heart! Every day when I go out I think of you and realize that I have never loved a woman in this world as much as I love you, o much desired rose. I am sure that you were destined to be mine.

This paean to her excellent qualities and beauty has the immediate effect of raising her to lofty heights, from which she claims she would fall, if their love were indeed fated. And if this should be the case, she reiterates in more specific terms her intention to become a nun:[23]

> Se distinata fosseti, – caderia de l'alteze,
> chè male messe forano – in teve mie belleze.
> Se tutto adivenissemi – tagliarami le treze
> e consore m'arenno a una magione
> avanti che m'artocchi 'n la persone.   (46–50)

If I were destined to be yours, I would fall from the heights, for my beauty would be badly placed in you. If all that should happen, I would cut my hair and become a nun in a convent before you could lay a hand on my body.

Again the *coblas capfinidas* technique of linking stanzas stresses the way the man uses her words to construct his own response: he would become a monk in order to be with her constantly:

> Se tu consore arenneti, – donna col viso cleri,
> a lo mostero venoci – e rennomi confleri:
> per tanta prova vencerti – faralo volonteri.
> Con teco stao la sera e lo maitino;
> besogn'è ch'io ti tegna al meo dimino.   (51–55)

If you become a nun, lady with the fair face, I will come to the

---

[23] See note 20 above.

monastery and become a monk. I would gladly do all I have to
do to win you. With you I will stay night and day: I must have
you in my possession.

This religiously incorrect response reinforces his dangerous nature, the risk he
poses to her as both an outsider (*istraniu*, 112) and a blasphemer. With all due
modesty, of course, she suggests that if he looks all over the world, he will
probably find at least one woman more beautiful than she:

> Boimé, tapina misera, – com'ao reo distinato!
> Gieso Cristo l'altissimo – del tutto m'è airato:
> concepistimi a abattere – in omo blestiemato.
>> Cerca la terra ch'este granne assai,
>> chiù bella donna di me troverai   (56–60)

> O woe is me, unfortunate wretch, how miserable is my destiny!
> Jesus Christ almighty is really mad at me: you (= Jesus) made
> me fall in with a blasphemer. Search throughout the whole wide
> world, you will find a lady more beautiful than I.

He warmly receives this proposal, but claims that he has already searched
throughout foreign lands and has not found her equal:

> Cercat'aio Calabr[ï]a, – Toscana e Lombardia,
> Puglia, Costantinopoli, – Genova, Pisa e Soria,
> Lamagna e Babilonïa – [e] tutta Barberia:
>> donna non [ci] trovai tanto cortese,
>> per che sovrana di meve te p[r]ese.   (61–65)

> I have searched Calabria, Tuscany, and Lombardy, Puglia, Con-
> stantinople, Genoa, Pisa and Syria, Germany and Babylon and
> all of Barbary: no woman have I found there of such courtesy,
> for which I have taken you to be my sovereign.

The broad scope of his epic journeys and his singular lack of success in this
great quest combine to impress upon the woman the seriousness of his interest
in her. Accordingly, she establishes the conditions under which she will grant him
her love: he must ask her hand in marriage from her parents and then marry her
in a public ceremony:

> Poi tanto trabagliasti[ti], – faccioti meo pregheri
> che tu vadi adomannimi – a mia mare e a mon peri.
> Se dare mi ti degnano, – menami a lo mosteri
>> e sposami davanti da la jenti;
>> e poi farò li tuo' comannamenti.   (66–70)

> Since you have worked so hard, I'll make you my request: that
> you go to my mother and father and ask for me in marriage. If
> they deign to give me to you, take me to the church and marry
> me in front of the people, and then I'll do what you command.

These steps – parental consent, public church wedding – follow standard matrimonial procedure in the period.[24] We should note that a number of literary anthologies, especially those for use in the public schools in Italy, end the poem at this point, as though to suggest, through omission, that these steps will be followed and that the two will marry and live happily ever after.[25] This is decidedly not the case; indeed, the *contrasto* moves ahead at a rapid pace with argument being met with counter-argument and with the introduction of new and ever more sexually suggestive images.[26] War imagery with its assortment of weapons and its terminology of assault and conquest is especially prevalent in the second part of the poem and emphasizes the sexual dimension. In one stanza (76–80), for example, the woman describes herself as a fortified castle ("forte castiello") and refers precisely to the war club, the "manganiello," which also signifies in this context the male sex organ. Along these same lines, the *contrasto* features the subtle play on the double meaning of "arma" ("soul" [*anima*] and "weapon"). At one point, the man states very clearly that he will never leave until he enjoys her sexual favors:

> Se morto essere deboci – od intagliato tutto,
> di quaci non mi mosera – se no ai[o] de lo frutto,
>   lo quale staci ne lo tuo jardino:
>   disïolo la sera e lo matino. (82–85)

> Even if I'm killed or cut completely up, I would not move from
> here, unless I have some of the fruit that is in your garden: I
> desire it night and day.

The fragrant rose of the first verse ("rosa fresca aulentissima") that became the delectable rose of the garden ("rosa fresca de l'orto," 13) has now been transformed into the fruit that is found in the woman's garden.

The woman continues to parry the man's verbal thrusts and to hold firm to her stated objective in this relationship: marriage. However, her earlier insistence on the various stages leading to the actual wedding ceremony has now been reduced to the man's simple swearing of a pledge on the Gospels to be her husband. This suggests the gradual weakening of her resolve under the constant barrage of his persuasive words: "S'a le Va[n]gele iurimi – che mi sia a marito, / avereme no poter' a sto monno" ("Unless you swear to me on the Gospels that you will be my husband, you will not have me in this world," 118–19).

In the final stanzas of the *contrasto* war imagery and metaphoric language

---

[24] See note 1 above.
[25] See, among others, Tommaso Casini, *Le origini e il Trecento*, vol. 1 of *Letteratura italiana, storia ed esempi per le scuole secondarie superiori* (Rome: Società Editrice Dante Alighieri, 1909); Giuseppe Lipparini, *Le pagine più belle della letteratura italiana*, vol. 1 (Milan: Signorelli, 1926); and Natalino Sapegno, *Scrittori d'Italia* (Florence: La Nuova Italia, 1972).
[26] There is even a reference to necrophilia in the *contrasto* (121–25). On this and other points concerning the erotic in early Italian literature, see my article, "Texts, Naked and Thinly Veiled: Erotic Elements in Medieval Italian Literature," in *Sex in the Middle Ages*, ed. Joyce E. Salisbury (New York: Garland, 1991), 83–109.

reach a crescendo. The man describes the extent of his devotion to her: so great is his desire for her that, if she should not satisfy it, he will cease his poetic activity, thus reinforcing the direct connection between sexual desire and poetic virtuosity and potency. His poetic talents and success depend completely on the inspiration provided by the woman and the thought of her joy, and should that source dry up, so to speak, so, too, would his artistry. The unifying thread of these concluding stanzas is the presence of the demonstrative *quisso* ("this" and its variants) that represents the complete joy of sexual solace, coitus:

> Se *quisso* non arcomplimi, – lassone lo cantare.
> Fallo, mia donna, plazzati, – che bene lo puoi fare.
>   Ancora tu no m'ami, molto t'amo,
>   sì m'ài preso come lo pesce a l'amo.
>   (132–135; emphasis mine)

If you don't do this for me, I'll stop singing and composing poetry. Do it, my lady, treat yourself, for you can certainly do it. While you may not yet love me, I really do love you. You have caught me like a fish on the hook.

The woman replies in kind to his entreaty and promises to give him what he wants, if he does what she asks:

> Sazzo che m'ami, [e] amoti – di core paladino.
> Levati suso e vattene, – tornaci a lo matino.
> Se ciò che dico facemi, – di bon cor t'amo e fino:
>   [eo] *quisso* ti 'mprometto sanza faglia,
>   te' la mia fede che m'ài in tua baglia.
>   (136–140; emphasis mine)

I know you love me, and I love you with a noble heart. Get up and go, return in the morning. If you do what I tell you, I will love you with a true and noble heart. This I promise you without fail: you have my word that you will have me in your power.

The war imagery reaches its climax with the man's request to the woman to kill him with "esto cortel novo" ("this new [or strange] knife," 142), for his soul / penis (*arma*) is becoming sad together with his heart ("che l'arma co l core mi si 'nfella," 145):

> Per zo che dici, carama, – neiente non mi movo;
> inanti prenni e scannami, – tolli esto cortel novo.
> *Sto* fatto fare potesi – inanti scalfi un uovo.
>   Arcompli mi' talento, [a]mica bella,
>   che l'arma co l core mi si 'nfella.
>   (141–145; emphasis mine)

No matter what you say, my dear, I'm not moving. Rather take this new/unusual knife and cut me up. You can do this deed

before you can cook an egg. Satisfy my desire, my love, for my
soul/weapon and my heart are in a sorrowful state.

Recognizing the distress of his *arma* ("weapon" / "soul"), the woman, departing
from her earlier demands of marriage, now asks only that the man swear on the
Gospels in order to have her. There is no mention of marriage, no pledge to be
her husband, just an oath to . . . love her (yes), to be faithful to her (of course), to
never disappoint her (certainly):

> Ben sazzo l'arma doleti – com'omo c'ave arsura.
> *Sto* fatto [far] non potesi – per null'altra misura
> se non a le Vangel[ï]e – che mo ti dico iura,
>> avereme non puoi in tua podesta;
>> inanti, prenni e tagliami la testa.
> > > > (146–150; emphasis mine)

Indeed I know your soul/weapon grieves you, like a man who
is burning. The only way that this deed can be done is for you
to swear on the Gospels; otherwise you cannot have me in your
power; rather take me and cut off my head.

The final two strophes present a rapid and sexually satisfying conclusion to the
events:

> Le Vangel[ï]e, carama? – ch'io le porto in sino!
> A lo mostero presile, – non ci era lo patrino.
> Sovr'esto libro iuroti – mai non ti vegno mino.
>> Arcompli mi' talento in caritate,
>> che l'arma me ne sta in suttilitate.
>
> Meo sire, poi iurastimi, – eo tutta quanta incenno;
> sono a la tua presenz[ï]a, – da voi non mi difenno.
> S'eo minespriso aioti, – merzè, a voi m'arenno.
>> A lo letto ne gimo a la bon'ura,
>> chè *chissa cosa* n'è data in ventura.
> > > > (151–160; emphasis mine)

The Gospels, my dear? I have them inside my shirt! I took them
from the monastery when the priest wasn't there. Upon this
book I swear to you that I will never disappoint you. Fulfill my
desire charitably for my soul/weapon is in a desperate state.
My lord, since you have sworn to me, I am burning all over; I
am here before you; I give myself to you. If I have not appreci-
ated you enough, please forgive me, I yield myself to you. Let's
go to bed quickly for this pleasure is given to us by good fortune.

The man swears over the stolen Gospels he *claims* to have hidden inside his shirt
(he never produces them!), and the oath that he pronounces is that he will never
fail or disappoint her; in short, he pledges to do precisely what she asked him to
(148), but there is no mention of marriage. In consequence to the swearing
ceremony, the woman commands that they go to bed immediately to consummate

their love. The conclusion, however, is far different from what might have been expected at the beginning of the poem, where marriage would seem to be the *sine qua non* for sexual intercourse. The chain of events does not lead to a marriage requested by the suitor, agreed to by the parents, performed by a priest, and witnessed by the populace. In short, Cielo d'Alcamo's *contrasto* stands in antithetical position to virtually all the poems examined in this essay in the sense that it presents how social codes of behavior are subverted. In the final analysis, the woman's insistence on marriage proves to be mere lip service to a social convention, which appears to be powerless and meaningless when confronted with urgent, natural sexual desires. This celebration of earthly desire and its consummation outside the bonds of marriage is similar to what we noted above in the discussion of the poem ("L'amor fa una donna amare") by Compagnetto da Prato. The elaborate structure of the *contrasto*, together with its highly nuanced language and vibrant sexual images, makes it one of the most highly developed and sustained poems of seduction and vibrant sexuality in early Italian poetry.

In conclusion, then, we have observed how these several poems articulate in a clear and insightful manner a variety of attitudes toward and approaches to the interrelated notions of coming of age, the rites of passage, and the question of marriage in thirteenth-century Italian literature. The poetic texts we have examined provide an interesting reflection of the operation of these physiological and psychological events within their socio-historical context. Further research into the so-called marginal voices and genres in medieval Italian literature promises to shed much needed light on the poetry of this important but all too frequently neglected period.

Some Pious Talk about Marriage: Two Speeches from the *Canterbury Tales*

Robert R. Edwards

> "Be war, ye wemen, of youre subtyl fo,
> Syn yit this day men may ensaumple se;
> And trusteth, as in love, no man but me."
>
> Geoffrey Chaucer, *Legend of Good Women*

> "Chaucer was evir – God wait – al womanis frend."
>
> Gavin Douglas, *The Aeneid of Vergil*

More than any other institution, marriage defined the roles of matrons and marginal women in medieval society. For matrons, it established the framework of personal, social, economic, political, and spiritual relations. The Middle English word "matron" is a later fourteenth-century borrowing from French that carries the accessory senses of a mature and respectable woman; its ultimate source, the Roman *matrona*, lends venerable authority to the associations the term seeks to invoke. For marginal women (a term whose origin and intellectual investments Barbara Hanawalt discusses in the first essay of this volume), marriage provided an inverse paradigm, a structure to identify difference and deviation: their marginality is, in a practical sense, what falls outside the sphere reserved for mature and respectable women. During the last quarter century, our understanding of medieval marriage and a matron's place within it has deepened and ramified, while marginality has claimed heightened attention not only for areas of cultural exclusion but also for what those areas can tell us about dominant formations. This is certainly not the place to summarize all we have learned, but a few general points are worth making as background for Chaucer's poetic representation of ideas about marriage and social relations.

The Scriptural warrant claimed for marriage in the Middle Ages, complicated as it is in the account of Genesis and in the traditions of Biblical, legal, and pastoral commentary, defines the nature of women by defining their role within marriage. Man (taking the term to include both sexes) is made in the image of God, while woman is identified as his helpmate. She thus comes into the world already gendered, socialized, and married. The medieval doctrine built on this warrant is a historical and cultural formation. Though doctrine claims to be transhistorical, given by God or Nature, multiple contexts – social, intellectual, religious, political, and economic – underlie its precepts. We might recall by way of example that St. Augustine, the most important early theorist of marriage for the Middle Ages, argues positions on marriage shaped in strong ways by contemporary polemics over Pelagianisn, Arianism, and Manicheanism.[1] Furthermore, theory and social practice exist in a dialectical relation. Modern scholars who have studied medieval marriage teach us, among other things, that these two dimensions are mutually defining. Whether one believes that ideas run before social change or that the discrepancies between precept and practice implicitly show the weakness or failure of doctrine, the essential point is that the two are dynamically connected.

This last point bears on the poetry of Geoffrey Chaucer, for it seems to me that the complex relation of doctrine and practice in the social sphere bears an important analogy to the relation between ideas and poetry. Chaucer does not make the ambitious claim of Renaissance Platonists that his works constitute a poetic heterocosm, a self-contained other world that reproduces reality, but he does find in books and poetry "these olde appreved stories" that are the source of our cultural memory and the occasion of moral speculation.[2] Moreover, in an intriguing passage early in the *Canterbury Tales* that seeks exculpation for speaking plainly, he suggests that the basis of authentic representation is the social habit of speech and conversation.

> Whoso shal telle a tale after a man,
> He moot reherce as ny as evere he kan
> Everich a word, if it be in his charge,
> Al speke he never so rudeliche and large,
> Or ellis he moot telle his tale untrewe,
> Or feyne thyng, or fynde wordes newe.   (I.731–36)

Here Chaucer claims a confident power for speech to embody truth, while he preserves his characteristic role of disingenuous narrator.[3] Unlike social practice, which alternately obscures and disguises its underlying foundations, literary discourse – what Chaucer calls telling a tale after a man – makes the conceptual

---

[1] See Elizabeth Clark, " 'Adam's Only Companion': Augustine and the Early Christian Debate on Marriage," in *The Olde Daunce: Love, Friendship, Sex, and Marriage in the Medieval World*, ed. Robert R. Edwards and Stephen Spector (Albany: State University of New York Press, 1991), 15–31. See Joseph J. Mogan, Jr., "Chaucer and the *Bona Matrimonii*," *Chaucer Review* 4 (1969–70): 123–41, for an application of Augustine's teachings on marriage to the *Canterbury Tales*.

[2] *Legend of Good Women* F 21, in *The Riverside Chaucer*, 3d ed., gen. ed. Larry D. Benson (Boston: Houghton Mifflin, 1987). All quotations from Chaucer will cite this edition.

[3] See Derek Pearsall, *The Canterbury Tales* (London: George Allen & Unwin, 1985), 31; and Winthrop Wetherbee, *Geoffrey Chaucer: The Canterbury Tales* (Cambridge: Cambridge University Press, 1989), 37, for useful remarks on the artistic and philosophical complexity of this passage.

grounding felt, hence accessible when ideas are put into language and performed by speakers in the world of the poetic text.

Throughout this century, critics have generally maintained that Chaucer introduced a debate on marriage into the fictional pilgrimage of the *Canterbury Tales*. Eleanor P. Hammond first broached this possibility in her discussion of the sequence of composition in the *Tales*.[4] George Lyman Kittredge, whose work represents the starting point of modern Chaucer criticism, elaborated Hammond's suggestion, proposing a discussion of marriage beginning with the Wife of Bath's Prologue and including the Clerk's Tale, Merchant's Tale, and Franklin's Tale. In this essay, I want to focus on passages from two tales usually thought to be opposite ends of the Marriage Group. The nadir of the marriage debate Kittredge took to be the Merchant's Tale, a story he described as "a frenzy of contempt and hatred." He found the resolution of the debate in the Franklin's Tale, which he believed to be identical with Chaucer's own view. "Certainly it is a solution," says Kittredge, "that does him infinite credit. A better has never been devised or imagined." [5] These two tales are sharply contrasted in their characters and outlook. In the Merchant's Tale, old January marries calculating young May, who betrays him in his love garden with his squire Damian. We feel little sympathy or attraction for the characters, and the world they inhabit is defined by human appetites and the ethos of the marketplace. The Franklin's Tale engages us, though not uncritically, with Arveragus and Dorigen's effort to create a marriage outside the medieval norm of mastery and domination, and we feel at least some measure of sympathy when the values on which their marriage is founded prove contradictory and confounding. For all these differences, however, the two tales share a remarkably similar structure. C. Hugh Holman describes them as the "recto and verso of the same page."[6] Both stories begin with a male character seeking marriage and proceed through a subordinate's declaration of love for the wife and a crisis of marital fidelity that is finally resolved. In both, a garden and external, mysterious forces are common elements. The tales also give us the speeches that I have called, in my title, some pious talk about marriage. It is talk, in each case, by men about women and marriage enlisting male authority; to this extent, it is

---

[4] Eleanor P. Hammond, *Chaucer: A Bibliographical Manual* (New York: Macmillan, 1908; reprint, New York: Peter Smith, 1933), 256.

[5] George Lyman Kittredge, "Chaucer's Discussion of Marriage," *Modern Philology* 9 (1911–12): 467; rpt. in *Chaucer Criticism, I: The "Canterbury Tales,"* ed. Richard Schoeck and Jerome Taylor, 2 vols. (Notre Dame, Ind.: Notre Dame University Press, 1960), 1: 145, 158. As John M. Manly suggested, the Monk was probably the pilgrim envisioned as the original speaker of the Merchant's Tale; see Helen Cooper, *The Canterbury Tales*, Oxford Guides to Chaucer (New York: Oxford University Press, 1989), 202–3. Donald R. Howard, "The Conclusion of the Marriage Group: Chaucer and the Human Condition," *Modern Philology* 57 (1959–60): 226, contends that the Franklin's solution to the problem of *maistrie* "is by no means the last word that could have been said on the subject of marriage. And it is unlikely to be all that Chaucer thought about it." He proposes that, depending on the order of tales one accepts, the Physician's Tale or Second Nun's Tale is a foil to the Franklin's Tale.

[6] C. Hugh Holman, "Courtly Love in the Merchant's and Franklin's Tales," *ELH* 18 (1951): 243.

a topic in current debates about who speaks for whom. Yet as I hope to show, it serves as a means for bringing to the surface and disclosing the conflicting cultural traditions that inform ideas about marriage.[7]

Chaucer introduces the long speech praising marriage (IV.1267–1392) at the start of the Merchant's Tale, just after he has described his singularly dislikable protagonist, the aging, lecherous Lombard knight January who determines to marry a young wife and find his earthly Paradise. Readers of the tale have traditionally assumed that the marriage encomium registers January's thoughts.[8] On this view, the encomium is a piece of extended rhetorical impersonation by which the Merchant, himself an unhappy husband of two months' standing, reports January's ideas on marriage and infects them with his own cynicism.[9] More recent readers contend, however, that the poem does not give adequate grounds for ascribing the speech to January and still less warrant for attributing it to the Merchant directly or even to Chaucer's persona.[10] The first line of the speech – "And certeinly, as sooth as God is kyng" – might plausibly be construed as a continuation of the lines quoted from January (1263–65); it reads equally well, however, as a transitional device for the speech. The line immediately after the encomium (1393) clearly signals a return to the narrative action rather than a continuation of an interior monologue. We have, then, a free-standing discourse about marriage, bracketed and suspended within the narrative, whose speaker the text leaves uncertain. The encomium is a tantalizing crux. The speech is self-contained except for two apparent editorializing asides, and it is generally self-consistent except for two lapses in its argument.[11] Chaucer achieves in the speech not indeterminacy but a kind of irreducibility, and it is this quality that reflects the tale's extraordinary balance between doctrine and literary representation.

---

[7] John M. Ganim, *Chaucerian Theatricality* (Princeton, N. J.: Princeton University Press, 1990) examines the play of voices and Bakhtinian dialogics in the *Canterbury Tales*. Ganim's concern is with the formal properties of the poem, especially the dispersion of the unity earlier critics saw in Chaucer and represented by visual metaphors for literary structure. By contrast, my interest in the performative voices of the text has to do with the substantive ethical questions the speeches address and with their capacity to reveal in the symbolic action of language the often contradictory assumptions of the speakers. This sense of talk differs from the ironic expectations that Bertilak's men have of Gawain – the "teccheles termes of talkyng noble" (917); *Sir Gawain and the Green Knight*, ed. J. R. R. Tolkien and E. V. Gordon, 2d ed. by Norman Davis (Oxford: Clarendon Press, 1972), 26.

[8] G. G. Sedgewick, "The Structure of *The Merchant's Tale*," *University of Toronto Quarterly* 17 (1947–48): 341, is the source for most subsequent views.

[9] Emerson Brown, Jr., "Biblical Women in the Merchant's Tale: Feminism, Antifeminism, and Beyond," *Viator* 5 (1974): 387.

[10] Donald R. Benson, "The Marriage 'Encomium' in the *Merchant's Tale*: A Chaucerian Crux," *Chaucer Review* 14 (1979–80): 48–60.

[11] Kittredge (452) points to the narratorial comments that a wife will last and endure "Wel lenger than thee list, paraventure" (1320) and that a couple will be so bound that no harm may befall them, "And namely upon the wyves syde" (1392). Donald R. Benson notes that the encomium's praise of wives as good and humble counselors is contradicted at one point: "She shal comande, and thou shalt suffren it, / and yet she wole obeye of curteisye" (1378–79). At another (1384–85), Paul's admonition that men should love their wives as the Church is misconstrued, says Benson, so that "in the *Merchant's Tale caritas* has become *cupiditas*" (57).

The pious statements praising marriage obviously invite an ironic reading, for in the end January is a blind cuckold, betrayed by his wife and squire in the garden he has constructed as the exclusive refuge of his pleasure. Yet none of the voices in the tale, not even that of the Merchant who seeks to draw us into his cynical perspective, is strong enough to claim the final authorial power to determine or limit the meaning of the speech. Quite apart from the tale's narrative strategies, the encomium retains a significant measure of orthodox marriage doctrine.

In composing the encomium, Chaucer drew chiefly on Eustache Deschamps's *Miroir de Mariage* and secondarily on Albertanus of Brescia's *Liber de amore Dei* and *Liber consolationis et consilii*.[12] St. Jerome's *Adversus Jovinianum* is the source for a misogynistic passage in the speech quoted from Theophrastus, which the speaker urges his readers to ignore.[13] The rhetorical structure that incorporates these sources borrows from the form of medieval sermons. Charles E. Shain and Donald R. Benson divide the encomium into three main parts, each with a theme praising wives: a wife is a glorious thing (1267–1310), a wife is God's gift (1311–36), and a wife is man's proof against adversity (1337–92).[14] The encomium is not a sermon proper, however; it lacks the expected partition of the *thema* or Scriptural quotation and the analytical elaboration of the parts.[15] Its rhetorical mode, as Benson notes, is "that of argument and exhortation" (54). The argument evolves over six major points, each amplified by recourse to authorities.[16]

1267–1310	To take a wife is a glorious thing
1311–18	A wife is God's gift
1319–36	Marriage is a sacrament
1337–46	A wife is a shield against adversity
1347–79	A wife offers a man good counsel
1380–92	A wife is a keeper of husbandry

[12] John Livingston Lowes, "Chaucer and the *Miroir de mariage*," *Modern Philology* 8 (1910–11): 168, observes, "the borrowings from Albertano constitute but a small portion even of the passage under discussion"; the longest passage is the series of *exempla* on women's counsel. He notes that Chaucer interweaves Albertanus and Deschamps, and concludes that Deschamps is the dominant influence (185–86). See *The Riverside Chaucer*, 884, for the compilation of Chaucer's sources; W. F. Bryan and Germaine Dempster, *Sources and Analogues of "Chaucer's Canterbury Tales"* (Chicago: University of Chicago Press, 1941), print only passages from Deschamps and Jerome, the latter in connection with the Wife of Bath's Prologue.

[13] Compare IV. 1296–1304 and Jerome 1.47, quoted in *Sources and Analogues*, 212.

[14] Donald R. Benson, 54; Charles E. Shain, "Pulpit Rhetoric in Three Canterbury Tales," *MLN* 70 (1955): 235–45. My account of these divisions is a composite of the two schemes. Benson sees the themes as stability and comfort (1267–1310), God's gift and sacrament of penance (1311–36), and wives as good counselors (1337–92); he also believes that the theme of the speech is contained in the third rather than the first division, an unusual arrangement in the *artes praedicandi*. Shain adds a fourth section of recapitulation (1383–92). These differences do not alter their fundamental agreement on the major divisions.

[15] For discussion of the *ars praedicandi*, see James J. Murphy, *Rhetoric in the Middle Ages: A History of Rhetorical Theory from St. Augustine to the Renaissance* (Berkeley: University of California Press, 1974), 269–355.

[16] Lowes; Carleton Brown, "The Evolution of the Canterbury 'Marriage Groups,' " *PMLA* 48 (1933): 1046; and John C. McGalliard, "Chaucer's *Merchant's Tale* and Deschamps' *Miroir*

As these divisions indicate, the encomium defines the nature of marriage by defining the nature of a wife. Her behavior is styled from the literature of domestic instruction, one of two or three competing social typologies in the Middle Ages (the others are misogyny and retirement to religious life). Wifehood is the functional equivalent in the speech to the social and spiritual institution of marriage. This blurring of distinctions contributes, of course, to the tale's comic and ironic power, but within the speech the arguments and appeals to authority suggest as well a normative view of marriage. Removed from January's indirect discourse or the Merchant's impersonation, the encomium reads in many respects as a set of orthodox homiletic assertions.[17] Elements of it reappear in the *Canterbury Tales*, notably in the Tale of Melibee and in the Parson's Tale, where we have little reason to suspect irony.[18]

A close look at the six parts of the encomium will show how Chaucer uses his sources for both conventional argument and poetic elaboration. The first assertion in the speech – to take a wife is a glorious thing – serves as its general theme. This proposition is a variation on Deschamps: "Mariage est moult bonne voye / Qui la prant en entencion / De faire generacion" (112–14).[19] Deschamps immediately associates marriage with fertility, inheritance, and the continuation of oneself and one's species. Chaucer abstracts his theme of marriage from the question of lineage, however; he treats engendering an heir as a special example of the merit of marriage "namely whan a man is oold and hoor" (IV.1269). In Deschamps, age is what lies ahead for his protagonist, Franc Vouloir, and what impels him to take steps to renew his form (124, 182, 196); in Chaucer, it is the accident that colors the representation of marriage. At the end of this section, Chaucer introduces a vignette of a buxom, attentive wife (1287–92), using Deschamps's portrayal of wifely succour (*Miroir* 221–30) and echoing the language of the marriage vows.[20] The portrait balances the sort of speech clerks

---

de mariage," *Philological Quarterly* 25 (1946): 193–220, discuss the sources, though some of the parallels they adduce seem remote. I differ from them specifically at 1267 and 1347.

[17] Michael D. Cherniss, "The *Clerk's Tale* and *Envoy*, the Wife of Bath's Purgatory, and the *Merchant's Tale*," *Chaucer Review* 6 (1971–72): 248, who finds a pervasive irony in the speech, allows that the speaker "is presenting a genuine ideal of what marriage ought to be." Derek Pearsall likewise remarks, "The matter of the encomium is orthodox, but there is an intermittent counter-current of irony which occasionally breaks the surface, in a manner uncharacteristic of Chaucer's own voice, in open sarcasm or in venomous aside" (196).

[18] In Melibee, Dame Prudence presents Rebecca, Judith, Abigail, and Esther in the same order as the Merchant and without evident irony as examples of women "ful discret and wis in conseillynge" (VII.1096). The encomium's Pauline admonition, "Love wel thy wyf, as Crist loved his chirche" (IV.1384; cf. Ephesians 5:25), reappears in the Parson's exposition of the remedies against lechery (X.929).

[19] *Oeuvres complètes de Eustache Deschamps*, ed. Gaston Raynaud, Société des anciens textes français, 11 vols. (Paris: Firmin Didot, 1878–1903), 9: 7. Lowes, 170 and Carleton Brown, 1046, cite *Miroir* 369–70 as the primary source: "Si fait bon avoir droicte ligne / Et espouser femme benigne." Both passages in Deschamps immediately connect marriage to questions of lineage.

[20] *Miroir* 224: "Son mari sert, baise et acole"; see Lowes, 170 and Carleton Brown, 1046. J. D. Burnley, "The Morality of *The Merchant's Tale*," *Yearbook of English Studies* 6 (1976): 19–20,

would supposedly improvise from Theophrastus, who argues that a friend or servant shows greater devotion than a wife.[21]

The second point made in the encomium – a wife is God's gift (1311) – is taken from Albertanus's *De amore Dei*. In the manuscripts of the Merchant's Tale, this begins a series of glosses that cite Scriptural and sapiential sources for the points made in the encomium.[22] In establishing the text of the *Canterbury Tales*, John M. Manly and Edith Rickert identified six groups of manuscripts recording the tale. Manuscripts in all six of these groups offer the gloss for the speech's second point: "Vxor est diligenda quia donum dei [est] Iesus filius Syrac domus et diuicie dantur a parentibus a domino autem proprie vxor bona vel prudens."[23] The third point – marriage is a sacrament (1319) – is asserted in the Parson's Tale (X.842, 883, 918), where it obviously stands as an orthodox expression of doctrine.[24] The encomium places a particular emphasis here on woman as *adiutorius* in marriage: "womman is for mannes helpe ywroght" (1324). The source is usually thought to be Albertanus's *Liber de amore Dei* (Lowes, 173). When Albertanus cites the relevant Biblical passage (Genesis 2:18) in the *Liber consolationis et consilii*, he has in mind the help of a woman's counsel.[25] Five of the six manuscript groups reproduce the Biblical passage in a gloss: "Faciamus ei adiutorium et extracta costa de corpore Ade fecit Euam et dixit propter hec

proposes the source in the language of the marriage service preserved in fourteenth-century vernacular manuals for occasional services.

[21] *Sources and Analogues*, 212; Deschamps repeats the arguments from Jerome in *Miroir* 1916–52.

[22] Emil Koeppel, "Chaucer und Albertanus Brixiensis," *Archiv für das Studium der neueren Sprachen und Litteraturen* 86 (1891): 41.

[23] John M. Manly and Edith Rickert, eds. *The Text of the Canterbury Tales*, 8 vols. (Chicago: University of Chicago Press, 1940), 3: 508–9, do not record that from their group I Harley 7335 (Ha⁵) has the gloss. They cite the following manuscripts and groups for the glosses in the encomium (2: 271–74):

I.	Tc2	Trinity College R.3.15 (595), Cambridge
II.	Hg	Hengwrt, National Library of Wales
	Ht	Hatton donat. 1, Bodleian Library
	Ra2	Rawlinson Poetry 149, Bodleian Library
	Ad3	Additional 35286, British Library
	Bo2	Bodley 686, Bodleian Library
III.	El	Ellesmere MS., Huntington Library
IV.	Dd	Dd.iv.24, University Library, Cambridge
	Cn	Cardigan MS, University of Texas Library
	Ma	English 113, John Rylands Library, Manchester
V.	Ch	Christ Church 152, Oxford
VI.	En3	Egerton 2864, British Library
	Ad1	Additional 5140, British Library

My quotation of the glosses will largely omit variants. Lawrence L. Besserman, "Chaucer and the Bible: The Case of the *Merchant's Tale*," *Hebrew University Studies in Literature* 6 (1978): 16, notes that the passage from Proverbs insists that a prudent wife is a gift from the Lord.

[24] See Siegfried Wenzel, ed. *Summa virtutum de remediis anime*, The Chaucer Library (Athens: University of Georgia Press, 1984), 22–23, 282–83.

[25] Albertanus of Brescia, *Liber consolationis et consilii*, ed. Thor Sundby, Chaucer Society 2d series, 8 (London: N. Trübner & Co., 1873), 17.

relinquet homo patrem et matrem et adherebit et cetera et erunt duo in carne vna." [26] Deschamps is the literary source for the final portion of this section, the claim that man and wife "moste nedes lyve in unitee. / O flessh they been, and o fleesh, as I gesse, / Hath but oon herte, in wele and in distresse" (1334–36). The *Miroir* characterizes marriage as a "tresdoulce conjunction": "Ce sont deux corps en union, / En une char par la loy joins, / Qui s'entraiment et près et loins" (217–20). Chaucer's elaboration adds Biblical overtones to Deschamps's ethical description. The Hengwrt manuscript marks the lines with "Nota" and adds in a later hand: "Vna caro vnum Animum in omni Adversitate cogitat."[27]

The second half of the encomium (1337–92) stresses the practical advantages of marriage in worldly affairs. Marriage forestalls adversity, and it does so in theory by proper domestic government. Deschamps proposes a differential of government: "Homs doit par dehors ordonner, / Femme doit dedenz gouverner" (221–22). He divides male and female spheres along the axes of ordering and governing, outside and inside (*Miroir* 231–40). World and home exist in a macrocosm-microcosm relation, yet each contains a genuine authority within its sphere. Chaucer's text, however, reformulates this division as wifely subordination. It also amplifies and redirects the meaning of the line "Elle se scet taire et souffrir" (238). In the original passage, this testifies to prudence more than compliance, but Chaucer transforms it into a short dialogue illustrating spousal obedience: "She seith nat ones 'nay,' whan he seith 'ye.' / 'Do this,' seith he; 'Al redy, sire,' seith she" (1345–46).

But if the encomium reasserts the marital politics of male priority, it reserves the most extensive treatment for female wisdom and counsel. Praising the "blisful ordre of wedlok precious" (1347), the speaker contends, "He may nat be deceyved, as I gesse, / So that he werke after his wyves reed" (1356–57).[28] Albertanus's *Liber consolationis et consilii* provides the argument ("tamen in multis invenitur optimum consilium"); it also gives the Biblical examples of virtuous wives and classical *sententiae* (from Seneca and Cato) that follow.[29] Manuscripts in four of Manly and Rickert's six groups, including Hengwrt and Ellesmere, furnish identifications for the Biblical wives (Rebecca, Judith, Abigail, and Esther) and texts for the proverbs by Seneca and Cato.[30] This dense

---

[26] Manly and Rickert's groups II–VI with same manuscripts as in note 23, above, and the addition of Ne (New College, D 314, Oxford) and Tc2 (Trinity College R.3.15 [595], Cambridge).

[27] Burnley, 21, derives the reference to "o flessh" (1335) from Genesis 2:24, Matthew 19:5–6, and Ephesians 5:22–33. Bo2 reads for line 1335: "O flessh they ben and o blode as y gesse" (fol. 115v).

[28] Lowes, 173, finds the source in *Miroir* 437 ("Si ne puez donc estre fraudez"). But in Deschamps's poem the advisers are speaking here of the care that his children will give Franc Vouloir in his old age, even if his wife has died.

[29] *Liber consolationis et consilii*, 17–19; cf. Koeppel, 36–37. *Miroir* 9107–49 discusses Judith and Esther as examples of chastity. The passage corresponding to this part of the encomium in the Tale of Melibee (VII.1097–1111) includes the list of comparisons that ends by valuing women for wisdom (cf. Albertanus, 18) but omits the classical proverbs; the source in this case is Renaud de Louens's translation and abridgement of the *Liber consolationis*; see *Riverside Chaucer*, 923.

[30] Manly and Rickert's groups II–V with same manuscripts as in note 23, above. From group

citation of authority reaches a culmination in the final section of the encomium (1380–92), which echoes the earlier theme of domestic government. "A wyf is kepere of thyn housbondrye" (1380), the speaker announces, paraphrasing Albertanus, who writes, "Bona mulier fidelis custos est et bona domus."[31] Albertanus in turn is quoting Petrus Alfonsi (*Disciplina clericalis* 15.11), but the rendering of *custos* and *domus* in Chaucer's text strongly echoes the passage from Deschamps used earlier to portray a wife's domestic government. The speech closes with paraphrases of St. Paul on loving one's wife and an admonition to "holden the siker weye" (1390).[32]

The encomium derives a significant hortatory power from these arguments and literary sources. Its initial theme of the glory of wedlock is supported by both spiritual sanction and practical, worldly wisdom. But the literary contexts of the encomium make it hard to read the speech merely in opposition to the Merchant's cynicism or as inadvertent truth uttered by the morally blind January. The Biblical wives, as many critics observe, offer good counsel tinged with deceit.[33] The intertextual relation to other sources complicates the picture further. As we have seen above, Chaucer shifts the emphases in some of the passages he adapts. The only assertion in the piece not traceable to literary sources is the one with the greatest potential for irony: "How myghte a man han any adversitee / That hath a wyf?" (1338–39).[34] Like January's blithe assumption that "wedlok is so esy and so clene, / That in this world it is a paradys" (1264–65), it looks forward to the tale's fabliau action and comic conclusion. Further, the passages Chaucer borrows from Deschamps, unlike Albertanus's didactic prescriptions, have their own poetic context. John Livingston Lowes claims that most of Chaucer's borrowings from Deschamps's *Miroir* concentrate in the first three thousand lines, especially the first thousand (181). If read for context as well as verbal echoes, their range narrows considerably.

Chaucer borrows chiefly from the speech in the *Miroir* given by the false friends of Deschamps's protagonist Franc Vouloir, who carry the names Folie, Desir, Faintise, and Servitute. In particular, Chaucer turns to their speech in Chapter Five on the general worth of marriage (*Miroir* 209–51). The advice these friends offer in favor of marriage is countered in Deschamps's poem by the misogynistic letter written by Repertoire de Science, and this finally inspires Franc Vouloir to seek spiritual rather than civil marriage. In other words, Chaucer takes his materials from the portion of the *Miroir* that Deschamps's poem sets out as a false view of marriage that ought to be rejected. If John C. McGalliard is

---

I, Ha5, fol. 114 provides the text of Cato's proverb, with the variant *sufferre* for *ferre*. From group VI, En3 and Ad1, the latter defective, provide the gloss for Jacob at 1362.

31 *Liber consolationis*, 19.

32 Manuscripts from the same groups as above (see note 23) furnish the texts from Paul in glosses. Manly and Rickert (3: 510) propose that the gloss in Tc2 derives from El and that Ne is probably independent.

33 See Brown, "Biblical Women" and Besserman, "Chaucer and the Bible."

34 Bo2 adds a gloss at 1342 ("If he be povre, she helpeth hym to swynke"): "vel drynke quod verum est et cetera." Dd adds at the same point: "or to drynke."

correct in claiming that the speech's reference to a wife as "paradys terrestre" derives from *Miroir* 815–17 but with the emphasis reversed (198–99), the intertextual relations again undercut the easy assertion of wifely obedience and virtue. For the passage in Deschamps comes from Franc Vouloir's own thoughts, and they warn against marriage: "Il me semble selon leurs diz / Ce n'est repos ne paradis, / Mais droiz enfers de tel riote" (*Miroir* 815–17). Finally, Richard Hazelton points out that the *sententia* about wifely advice from Cato by way of Albertanus functions as parody. Chaucer, he notes, suppresses the essential qualification about proper, honest, or virtuous (*frugi*) advice: "Uxoris linguam, si frugi est, ferre memento." Hazelton proposes that Chaucer's omission is "a detail in the artistry that transforms Albertano's sterile and pedantic marshalling of authorities into its comic antithesis."[35] Chaucer's early readers, it seems, were eager to restore the qualification he suppressed. The same manuscript groups that supply the earlier Biblical texts and the text of Seneca furnish the full text of Cato in a gloss.[36]

Now, just as we cannot clearly locate the speaker of the encomium, we cannot establish whether Chaucer also borrows Deschamps's irony or turns to the friends' speeches solely for their themes and *topoi*. But we can judge the aesthetic effect. The propositions about marriage offered in the speech are deeply ambivalent and problematic, and they function in a way consistent with Chaucer's mature artistry. Normative and orthodox in themselves, they emanate, like the truth of the Pardoner's Tale, from bad advisers and speak to January's principal concerns – property and dominance. Yet their meaning is only partly determined by the tale's subsequent action. Because the encomium stands apart from January and the Merchant, it offers a view of marriage that retains a measure of its doctrinal meaning and thereby resists the effort to discredit it. The Merchant's narration and the marriage encomium, though presented in the tale as separate levels of discourse, are connected in an aesthetic dialectic that Chaucer does not seek to resolve so much as intensify.

The marriage encomium has a close partner in a second speech from the Marriage Group, which likewise affords us a view of marriage doctrine performed in language and eventually set against narrative action. In his tale of Arveragus and Dorigen, the Franklin seems to portray a modern marriage evolving away from conventional institutional structures based on a husband's governance and a wife's subordination. Arveragus's wooing embodies the courtly elements of service and "meke obeysaunce" (V.739). When Dorigen accepts him, she takes him "for hir housbonde and hir lord, / Of swich lordshipe as men han over hir wyves" (742–43), but the coercive aspect of a husband's "lordship" is quickly mitigated. Arveragus freely elects not to exercise "maistrie" and to follow and obey his wife so long as he retains the facing-saving fiction of dominance – "Save that the name of soveraynetee, / That wolde he have for shame of his degree"

---

[35] Richard Hazelton, "Chaucer and Cato," *Speculum* 35 (1960): 376. Hazelton argues that Chaucer generally uses Cato for parody.

[36] Groups II–V, with one witness (Ha5) for group I.

(751–52).[37] Responding to this liberality, Dorigen pledges precisely the marital accord that the Wife of Bath grants after she has secured "By maistrie, al the soveraynetee" (III.818) over her fifth husband. Thus Arveragus and Dorigen strike "an humble, wys accord" (791) in which Arveragus fulfills the dual roles of "Servant in love, and lord in mariage" (793).

It is at this point that the Franklin intrudes with his speech on marital values (761–91). His speech appears at the same structural position as the marriage encomium in the Merchant's Tale – just after he has introduced his characters and established the fictional premise of the narrative. The Franklin begins the speech with a vocative signaling his authorship. He addresses his audience of pilgrims (or at least those of the appropriate rank and gender) as "sires" (V.761).[38] Except for this single marker, his speech stands as an independent discourse on ethics and erotic values; and like the marriage encomium, it is inserted as a rhetorical amplification that retards the pace of the narrative. It offers as well a set of terms for reading the narrative, though the terms are as much at issue as the tale.

The Franklin's speech on love is organized around the themes of friendship, patience, and temperance. These themes form an apparently cohesive set of values that privilege mutual obligations over dominance and promise stability and the power to make accommodations. Friends are bound to respect one another's wishes, the Franklin tells us, and their bond of love is opposed to the exercise of individual power through *maistrie*. Patience allows for the adjustments required to maintain love and friendship.[39] It also allows a margin of discretion in human experience. As the Franklin explains, many factors – some internal, others beyond human control – lead to transgressions and torts: "Ire, siknesse, or constellacioun, / Wyn, wo, or chaungynge of complexioun / Causeth ful ofte to doon amys or speken" (V.781–83). Mary Carruthers observes, "Patience is a form of generosity as the Franklin defines it, the ability to forgive human weakness and to respond with equanimity to the hasty words or ill-conceived actions of others."[40] Jill Mann says, "The ideal of patience better befits the way human beings are, because the simplest and most fundamental truth about people, for Chaucer, is that they change" (140) and that human relations are therefore dynamic. Another value of patience is that it frees one from the oppressive burden of justice and from cycles of vengeance: "On every wrong a man may nat be wreken" (784). Implicit in patience is temperance, the third element. Temperance, the Franklin says, requires a capacity for judgment, for knowing when to exercise restraint. He makes

---

[37] John Fyler, "Love and Degree in the *Franklin's Tale*," *Chaucer Review* 21 (1986–87): 323, contends (rightly, I believe) that the phrase "shame of his degree" refers to Arveragus's comparatively low social degree.

[38] Jill Mann, "Chaucerian Themes and Style in the *Franklin's Tale*," in *Medieval Literature: Chaucer and the Alliterative Tradition*, ed. Boris Ford, vol. 1, pt. 1 of the New Pelican Guide to English Literature (Harmondsworth, Middlesex: Penguin, 1982), 137, reads "sires" as part of Chaucer's appeal to general experience. In the context of the headlink to the Squire's Tale, it seems likely that the Franklin has in mind here gentlemen of noble rank, actual or presumptive.

[39] En3 contains two glosses on the speech: "pacientes vincunt" (774) and "disce pati" (778).

[40] Mary J. Carruthers, "The Gentilesse of Chaucer's Franklin," *Criticism* 23 (1981): 296.

temperance a form of practical reason, which his characters seek to demonstrate. For the purpose of living in "ese," Arveragus promises "suffrance" (788), which evidently combines patience and temperance, and he receives in return a pledge of fidelity from Dorigen.

On the surface at least, the Franklin's speech seems to redefine love away from appetite and power and toward an ideal of reciprocity that incorporates enough moral latitude and worldly wisdom to be practicable. It is in one sense a theory of marriage acutely aware of human flaws and the complexity of living in a fallen world. Kittredge believed the speech incorporated both love and *gentilesse* (155). Subsequent critics have interpreted it variously as a triumph over selfishness, an effort to level inequalities, or a preparation for the story's ending.[41] Kathryn Jacobs has seen in the speech a capacity to resign individual interests in favor of others, and she takes marriage as a metaphor here for other social relations.[42] John Fyler regards it as an evocation of the Golden Age, before hierarchies appeared in human institutions (330, 333). Mann, emphasizing the central value of patience, argues that the Franklin's ideal is dynamic, not static because it is based "on alternation in the exercise of power and the surrender of power" by the marriage partners (139).

These views are nonetheless challenged by quite different responses to the speech. J. Terry Frazier argues that the speech is a digression with no functional value in the tale.[43] Most critics who reject the speech tend to follow one of two lines. D. W. Robertson, Jr., and others attack the speech on doctrinal grounds, contending that Arveragus's resignation of *maistrie* over his wife is precisely what authoritative figures like the Parson (X.926) warn against.[44] Russell A. Peck writes, "Frustration and confusion follow Dorigen and Arveragus's mis-oriented marriage as dusk does the day."[45] Alternatively, the speech is dismissed because the events of the story seem to belie the claim that Arveragus has resigned *maistrie*. Invoking the sententious claim "Trouthe is the hyeste thyng that man may kepe" (1479), he directs his wife, "Ye shul youre trouthe holden" (1474) and sends her off to keep the rash promise she has made in play to give her love to another man.[46]

[41] See the characterization of critical positions in *The Riverside Chaucer*, 897.

[42] Kathryn Jacobs, "The Marriage Contract of the *Franklin's Tale*: The Remaking of Society," *Chaucer Review* 20 (1985–86): 132–43.

[43] See J. Terry Frazier, "The Digression on Marriage in *The Franklin's Tale*," *South Atlantic Bulletin* 43 (1978): 75–85. Clair C. Olson, "The Interludes of the Marriage Group in the *Canterbury Tales*," in *Chaucer and Middle English Studies in Honour of Rossell Hope Robbins*, ed. Beryl Rowland (Kent, Ohio: Kent State University Press, 1974), 165, argues for a similar disjunction: "In the *Franklin's Tale*, the idea of magnanimity between husband and wife is introduced in an abstract passage of forty-one lines near the beginning (V, 761–802), but is not emphasized at the end."

[44] D. W. Robertson, Jr., *A Preface to Chaucer* (Princeton, N.J.: Princeton University Press, 1962), 470–71.

[45] Russell A. Peck, "Sovereignty and the Two Worlds of the *Franklin's Tale*," *Chaucer Review* 1 (1966–67): 256.

[46] Wolfgang E. H. Rudat, "*Gentilesse* and the Marriage Debate in the Franklin's Tale:

The problems of the Franklin's speech do not arise merely because it contradicts the Parson's orthodoxy or the subsequent action of the story. They have to do in part with Chaucer's project of translating Boccaccio's aristocratic story into a wholly different sensibility – namely, the social aspirations of a narrator whose actual standing in the fourteenth century may hover uncertainly among the lower nobility, though few critics are inclined nowadays to see him as bourgeois.[47] It is worth remembering that neither the unnamed husband in Boccaccio's *Filocolo* nor Gilberto in *Decameron* 10.5 gives any indication at all of resigning mastery over their wives. Chaucer adds through the character of the Franklin both the disquisition on marriage and friendship and the agreement by which Arveragus is a servant in love and only a nominal lord in marriage. In the *Filocolo*, the husband seems not to agonize over the loss of the wife's chastity but insists on her fulfilling the bargain and not repeating her error. In the *Decameron*, Gilberto suggests that there may be some unacknowledged desire in Dianora's heart which led to her rash promise. He warns about the erotic potential of language: "Le parole per gli orecchi dal cuore ricevute hanno maggior forza che molti non stimano, e quasi ogni cosa diviene agli amanti possibile" ("Words received through the ears by the heart have more power than many people believe, and almost everything becomes possible for lovers").[48] Dianora acted wrongly, he says, first in listening to the suitor and then in bargaining with him. He wants her to seek a release from the promise if she can protect her chastity; failing that, she may give her body one time but not her heart.

Still, the most revealing problems are internal to the speech. Robert P. Miller has argued that the speech should be read against the views presented by Reason in the *Roman de la Rose* and ultimately by Lady Philosophy in Boethius's

---

Chaucer's Squires and the Question of Nobility," *Neophilologus* 68 (1984): 460, points out that Arveragus's promise to Dorigen is that he will "upon hym take no maistrie / Agayn her wyl" (747–48). Rudat proposes that Arveragus holds to a strict reading of the stipulation and that Dorigen manipulates him to save herself after she has been outwitted by Aurelius. Gerhard Joseph, "The *Franklin's Tale*: Chaucer's Theodicy," *Chaucer Review* 1 (1966–67): 22, contends that because Arveragus abrogates all sovereignty to Dorigen, she is unprepared to face adversity. Robert E. Kaske, "Chaucer's Marriage Group," in *Chaucer the Love Poet*, ed. Jerome Mitchell and William Provost (Athens: University of Georgia Press, 1973), 63–64, proposes that in the end Arveragus rules Dorigen not by dominance but by "outthinking" her and that he sends her to Aurelius (certain he will not exact the promise) in order to teach her a lesson in prudence. This reading of Aurelius's motives does not explain why Arveragus breaks into tears after asserting the high value of *trouthe* (V.1480). Traugott Lawler, *The One and the Many in the "Canterbury Tales"* (Hamden, Conn.: Archon Books, 1980), 78, rightly observes that one way to read the action is that "Arveragus, so far from abandoning maistrie, treats his wife as a possession to be shared or not shared."

[47] Carruthers and Fyler argue that the social line separating the Franklin from the Squire and Knight had been effectively erased – or obscured – in Chaucer's day. See also Henrik Specht, *Chaucer's Franklin in the Canterbury Tales: The Social and Literary Background of a Chaucerian Character* (Copenhagen: Akademisk Forlag, 1981); and Caroline D. Eckhardt, "Chaucer's Franklin and Others of the Vavasour Family," *Modern Philology* 87 (1990): 239–48.

[48] Giovanni Boccaccio, *Il Decameron*, ed. Vittore Branca, vol. 4 of *Tutte le opere di Giovanni Boccaccio*, gen. ed. Vittore Branca, 12 vols. (Verona: Mondadori, 1964–83), 4: 880.

Consolatio Philosophiae.[49] I propose that the problems derive even more profoundly from the sources and tradition to which Chaucer turned for thematic elaboration.[50] The Franklin believes that the mutual obligations of marriage partners depend on the rejection of *maistrie*. He thus opposes the realignment of sovereignty in marriage in the Wife of Bath's Prologue and Tale, where women are presumably on top but the structure of domination remains intact. Taking friendship as the model for love, he implies that the renunciation of husbandly domination leads necessarily to the mutuality of friendship. It is for him a necessary and sufficient cause, and he does not entertain the possibility that the absence of domination might not of itself compel mutuality. "Love wol nat been constreyned by maistrye" (764), the Franklin confidently asserts. In so doing, he repeats the neo-Ovidian advice of Ami to the Lover in the *Rose*:

> "Car il convient amors morir
> Quant amant vuelent seignorir.
> Amors ne puet durer ne vivre
> Se n'est en cuer franc et delivre."

> "[L]ove must die when lovers want lordship. Love cannot endure or live if it is not free and active in the heart."[51]

This advice comes at a point in the *Rose* that has a particular resonance for the Franklin's Tale. As with the use of Deschamps's *Miroir* in the Merchant's Tale, context bears on meaning. Ami has just finished a long speech imitating a jealous, dominating husband, and soon he will describe the problems that occur when a man stops being a servant in love and becomes a lord in marriage. At this moment, he says that the way to forestall such problems is to follow the practice of the ancients who conducted friendship without dominance or economic exchange:

> "Por ce, compains, li ancien,
> Sans servitute et sans lien,
> Pesiblement, sans vilonnie,
> S'entreportoient compaignie. . . ."

> "It was for this reason, my friend, that the ancients maintained

---

[49] Robert P. Miller, "The Epicurean Homily on Marriage by Chaucer's Franklin," *Mediaevalia* 6 (1980): 151–86.

[50] The analysis I offer here does not consider the Franklin's character or his social status. Critical opinion has moved back and forth between praise and dismissal of the Franklin. Kittredge is straightforward in valuing the Franklin and his announced precepts. Alan T. Gaylord, "The Promises in *The Franklin's Tale*," *ELH* 31 (1964): 321–45, and "From Dorigen to the Vavasour: Reading Backwards," in *The Olde Daunce*, 177–200; and D. W. Robertson, Jr., "Chaucer's Franklin and his Tale," *Costerus* 1 (1974): 1–26, exemplify a prevalent skepticism about the Franklin as a moral spokesman. A reaction to the skeptical view of the Franklin appears in Jill Mann, 133–53; Pearsall, 144–60; and Cooper, 230–45.

[51] *Le Roman de la Rose*, ed. Daniel Poirion (Paris: Garnier-Flammarion, 1974), lines 9439–42; *The Romance of the Rose*, trans. Charles Dahlberg (Princeton, N. J.: Princeton University Press, 1971), 170.

their friendship for each other without bonds of servitude, peaceably, and without boorishness. . . ." (9493–96).[52]

The Franklin's speech gives a different formulation from Jean de Meun's evocation in this passage of a Golden Age before hierarchy, differentiation, and monetary exchange. Ami hints at the idea of medieval theologians and canonists that a wife is to be regarded as a *socia*, a companion equal in standing but subordinate with respect to succession because she was made after Adam.[53] The Franklin, by contrast, goes to the doctrine espoused by the Old Woman later in the *Roman de la Rose*, who claims,"women are born free" (13875):

> "[Nature] Ains nous a fait, biau fix, n'en doutes,
> Toutes por touz et touz por toutes,
> Chascune por chascun commune
> Et commun chascun por chascune."

> "Instead, fair son, never doubt that [Nature] has made all us women for all men and all men for all women, each woman common to every man and every man common to each woman." (13885–88) [54]

Instead of an argument for mutual obligation and reinforcing virtue, the Franklin invokes natural appetite, which operates across the species and leads to fragmentation and dominance rather than accord. The "liberty" he extols has its roots in the biological compulsion of creaturely desire; it is "freedom from constraint" rather than freedom for the goods of marriage.[55]

As the *Rose* makes explicit, the tradition behind Ami's prescription for friendship in love is classical, not medieval. It thus proceeds on significantly different assumptions from the Franklin's idea of equality and mutuality, particularly as regards social relations. In Aristotle's *Nicomachean Ethics* and Cicero's *De amicitia*, friendship is possible between equals, and the model they have in mind

---

[52] Roger S. Loomis, "A Parallel to the Franklin's Discussion of Marriage," in *Philologica: The Malone Anniversary Papers*, ed. Thomas A. Kirby and Henry Bosley Woolf (Baltimore: Johns Hopkins Press, 1949), 191–94, suggests that the association of a wife as *amie* and *dame* appears in Arthurian romance as early as Chrétien de Troyes.

[53] Here Jean de Meun invokes the "rib-topos" from medieval marriage doctrine, by which authorities like Augustine, Bernard of Clairvaux, Hugh of St. Victor, Aelred of Rievaulx, and Robert de Sorbon fashioned the wife as a *socia* rather than inferior; see Erik Kooper, "Loving the Unequal Equal: Medieval Theologians and Marital Affection," in *The Olde Daunce*, 44–56.

[54] Joanne Rice's notes in *The Riverside Chaucer*, 896, stress the Boethian formulation of liberty slightly later in the Old Woman's speech. Dean Spruill Fansler, *Chaucer and the Roman de la Rose* (New York: Columbia University Press, 1914), 194, 220, proposes sources elsewhere in the poem that seem remote from the Franklin's discussion.

[55] Raymond P. Tripp, Jr., "The Franklin's Solution to the 'Marriage Debate,' " in *New Views on Chaucer: Essays in Generative Criticism* (Denver: Society for New Language Study), 37–38, proposes that the line "Women, of kynde, desiren libertee" can be taken in two senses: women naturally want to be free and women want to be free of their biological compulsions (taking "of kynde" to modify "libertee" rather than "desiren"). Miller, 170–74, contends that the passage is built on a view of man's fallen nature and on Boethian false felicity.

involves freeborn, noble males. When Cicero's Laelius recalls his friendship with Scipio, he describes sharing public and private concerns, domiciles and military campaigns, and a common outlook: "id in quo omnis vis est amicitiae, voluntatum studiorum sententiarum summa consensio" ("the whole essence of friendship [is] the most complete agreement in policy, in pursuits, and in opinions").[56] Laelius affirms as a first principle that friendship can exist only between good men: "Sed hoc primum sentio, nisi in bonis amicitiam esse non posse" (126). *Bonis* in this case means "aristocracy." He gives a definition of friendship that might apply generally to Arveragus and Dorigen's marriage: "Est enim amicitia nihil aliud nisi omnium divinarum humanarumque rerum cum benevolentia et caritate consensio" ("friendship is nothing else than an accord in all things, human and divine, conjoined with mutual goodwill and affection" [130–31]). But it is clear from his examples that the accord (*consensio*) is between men.

Friendship is also problematic in the Franklin's speech because the Franklin applies a different aim to the Ciceronian ideal. Cicero envisions friendship as a "honesta certatio" (9.32), a rivalry of virtue. In a long discussion, he points out that one does not enter friendship with an eye toward gaining worldly advantages or compensating for deficiencies. Virtue drives friendship. By way of example, he says of his bond to Scipio: "ego admiratione quadam virtutis eius, ille vicissim opinione fortasse non nulla quam de meis moribus habebat, me dilexit" ("I loved him because of a certain admiration for his virtue, and he, in turn, loved me, because, it may be, of the fairly good opinion which he had of my character" [142–43]). By contrast, Arveragus undertakes his novel marriage for the purposes that Cicero flatly discredits: he wants "To lyve in ese" (788). He and Dorigen seek a life of "prosperitee" (804), a term that the Clerk's Tale has earlier made ambiguous and the Merchant's Tale robbed of any moral standing. The objective for Arveragus and Dorigen comes closest to what the twelfth-century writer Aelred of Rievaulx called "worldly friendship": a bond "born of a desire for temporal advantage or possessions" rather than spiritual friendship resembling Ciceronian virtue.[57]

In these two speeches from the Merchant's Tale and the Franklin's Tale, Chaucer gives us some pious talk about marriage as a way of prefacing and reflecting on his stories. Both speeches obviously have a complex relation to the tellers and their narratives. The marriage encomium hovers as free discourse, neither January's thought nor the Merchant's ironic premise. The Franklin's speech is in some respect a demonstration of character, the use of *oratio* to show the inner man (*homo interior*), but it is a tale told after a man as he presents himself to others.[58]

---

[56] Cicero, *De senectute, de amicitia, de divinatione*, ed. and trans. William Armistead Falconer, Loeb Classical Library (Cambridge, Mass.: Harvard University Press, 1923), 124–25.

[57] Aelred of Rievaulx, *Spiritual Friendship*, trans. Mary Eugenia Laker, Cistercian Fathers Series 5 (Kalamazoo, Mich.: Cistercian Publications, 1974), 60. Aelred closely follows Cicero but distinguishes carnal, worldly, and spiritual friendship; for recent discussion, see Kooper.

[58] Matthew of Vendôme's *Ars versificatoria*, 1.74 uses the techniques of character description outlined in Cicero's *De inventione*, 1.24–25 and adds examples from Thierry of Chartres's *Commentarius super Libros De Inventione*. For Matthew, see Edmond Faral, *Les arts poétiques*

The tales following the speeches give distinctly paradoxical illustrations of their doctrines. January is betrayed by his wife and squire, but it is not clear whether they fool him or he chooses to countenance their infidelity. Arveragus's gesture of maintaining *trouthe* gains the admiration of the squire who would betray him and of the clerk whose powers have made the impossible task the cause of marital crisis. But the Franklin's final question about his characters – "Which was the mooste fre" (V.1622) – speaks only about the men, and it takes for granted a structure of values whose social differences marriage seems to replicate.[59] Dorigen, in any case, is not a plausible answer to the question. What Chaucer does artistically in both speeches is to prepare us for the richness and moral complication of his stories. By putting doctrine into speech and relating speech to narrative action, he gives a habitation and agency to the central ideas of his culture. The point is not that he cancels out medieval marriage doctrine by showing that it is hopelessly, even perniciously constituted against itself. Rather, the speeches like the stories claim a territory for our moral imagination, where we can judge the prescriptions of doctrine and examine human action, spoken and performed.

---

du XIIe et du XIIIe siècle (Paris: Champion, 1924), 135–36. For Thierry, see *The Latin Rhetorical Commentaries of Thierry of Chartres*, ed. Karin M. Fredborg (Toronto: Pontifical Institute of Mediaeval Studies, 1988), 13.

[59] Stephen Knight, "Ideology in 'The Franklin's Tale,' " *Parergon* 28 (1980): 16, contends that Chaucer "brings the value of generosity explicitly close to a matter of birth and aristocracy" and so goes against the theme developed by the Wife of Bath.